A Week of Simple Offices

A Week of Simple Offices

Edited by

Michael Boag, Jonathan Brown,

Paula Sonley, Nicolas Stebbing CR

and Adam Wilson

Community of the Resurrection

Mirfield

The editors are most grateful to Fr Peter Allan CR, the Reverend Wealands Bell, Fr George Guiver CR and Br Tristram SSF for their kind assistance.

Also in this series:
Simple Offices: Saints and Seasons 2001

A Week of Simple Offices
Compiled by Jonathan Brown.
Designed and typeset by Michael Boag.

ISBN 0 902834 20 7

A CIP catalogue record for this book is available from the British Library.

Printed in England by Page Bros (Norwich) Ltd.

First published Easter 2000,
second impression Ascension 2000,
third impression Pentecost 2002

Mirfield Publications,
House of the Resurrection,
Mirfield,
West Yorkshire WF14 0BN.

Contents

Διὰ πάσης προσευχῆς καὶ δεήσεως
προσευχόμενοι ἐν παντὶ καιρῷ
ἐν πνεύματι

Pray at all times in the Spirit,
with all prayer and supplication
Ephesians 6.18

A Week of Simple Offices

IN RECENT YEARS more and more Christian people have recognised the value of a daily office—morning and evening prayer drawn largely from the psalms and Holy Scripture. Most often they pray these offices alone, at home, on the way to work, or even on holiday. Yet we never really pray alone, for in the offices we join with the prayer of the whole Christian Church. Many different office books now exist, trying to meet different needs and expressing the reality of membership in different families of Christian people.

In this little collection of morning and evening prayer drawn directly from the CR Office we hope that our friends will find a simple but enduring form of prayer which will join them with us in the prayer that we offer in our Community chapels. This will strengthen the support we give each other and increase the worship offered to God through our Lord Jesus Christ on behalf of the world in which we live.

Praying the Office

Each office in this little book is complete in itself. The only alternatives are the two scriptural readings, only one of which need be read. We hope that the familiarity gained over several weeks or months of using the same material will deepen understanding and engender love for these fragments of Holy Scripture. The psalms and canticles offered are all set for the day of the week on which they are used in the Community.

The offices can be read silently, or recited aloud, or sung, alone or with others. If they are said at home it may be very helpful to light a candle and place a postcard by the candle to remind you of a holy place or a picture which speaks of God and to create an atmosphere that helps to focus the mind.

The morning office begins always with *O Lord open our lips*. Without God we would not exist. Without the life given by the Holy Spirit, we could never breathe. Without him we cannot pray. It is the Holy Spirit praying within us who brings us to take part in Christ's eternal prayer to the Father. So I am not alone. God is praying in me.

This verse has traditionally been linked with the Resurrection. God has raised us from sleep, has raised us too from the sleep of sin, and will raise us up and open our lips when we have finally passed through death. In saying these words we participate now in his eternal life.

In the evening office we begin with *O God make speed to save us*. Again we need God's help in order to pray. Without him we can do nothing. So at the end of the day, before we attempt to pray we cry,

"Help!" With these words we are saying that this moment of prayer is not just our own private concern—it is opening a door for God to start praying in us for the salvation of his world, and in him we can place our absolute trust.

Psalms and canticles should be said slowly and reflectively and at the end of each there may be a pause in which a brief prayer can be offered to God. The custom of saying *Glory to the Father and to the Son and to the Holy Spirit, as it was in the beginning, is now and shall be for ever, Amen* at the end of psalms and canticles is part of this ancient practice. Before the final Collect there may also be a few minutes of intercession, then all is summed up in the prayer which Jesus taught us.

The material in the last few pages of this book may be used instead of what is provided or may be found to be a useful addition to prayer when time permits.

Sunday Morning

O Lord open our lips.
  And our mouth shall proclaim your praise.

Hymn *Rejoice, the Lord is King*

Rejoice, the Lord is King,
Your Lord and King adore;
Mortals, give thanks and sing,
And triumph evermore:
  Lift up your heart, lift up your voice;
  Rejoice, again I say, rejoice!

Jesus, the Saviour, reigns,
The God of truth and love;
When he had purged our stains,
He took his seat above:

He sits at God's right hand
Till all his foes submit,
And bow to his command,
And fall beneath his feet:
  Lift up your heart, lift up your voice;
  Rejoice, again I say, rejoice!

Psalm 110 *Dixit Dominus*

1 The Lord said to my lord,
    "Sit at my right hand, *
  until I make your enemies your footstool."
2 The Lord will send the sceptre
    of your power out of Zion, *
  saying, "Rule over your enemies
    round about you.
3 Princely state has been yours
    from the day of your birth, *
  in the beauty of holiness have I begotten you,
    like dew from the womb of the morning."
4 The Lord has sworn and he will not recant: *
  "You are a priest for ever
    after the order of Melchizedek."
5 The Lord who is at your right hand
    will smite kings in the day of his wrath; *
  he will rule over the nations.
6 He will heap high the corpses; *
  he will smash heads over the wide earth.
7 He will drink from the brook
    beside the road; *
  therefore he will lift high his head.

Psalm 111 *Confitebor tibi*

1 Hallelujah!
I will give thanks to the Lord
with my whole heart, *
in the assembly of the upright,
in the congregation.
2 Great are the deeds of the Lord! *
they are studied by all who delight in them.
3 His work is full of majesty and splendour, *
and his righteousness endures for ever.
4 He makes his marvellous works
to be remembered; *
the Lord is gracious and full of compassion.
5 He gives food to those who fear him; *
he is ever mindful of his covenant.
6 He has shown his people
the power of his works *
in giving them the lands of the nations.
7 The works of his hands
are faithfulness and justice; *
all his commandments are sure.
8 They stand fast for ever and ever, *
because they are done in truth and equity.
9 He sent redemption to his people;
he commanded his covenant for ever; *
holy and awesome is his name.

10 The fear of the Lord
is the beginning of wisdom; *
those who act accordingly
have a good understanding;
his praise endures for ever.

Luke 24.1–9

On the first day of the week, at early dawn, they went to the tomb, taking the spices which they had prepared. And they found the stone rolled away from the tomb, but when they went in they did not find the body. While they were perplexed about this, behold, two men stood by them in dazzling apparel; and as they were frightened and bowed their faces to the ground, the men said to them, "Why do you seek the living among the dead? Remember how he told you, while he was still in Galilee, that the Son of man must be delivered into the hands of sinful men, and be crucified, and on the third day rise." And they remembered his words, and returning from the tomb they told all this to the eleven and to all the rest.

John 20.11–18

But Mary stood weeping outside the tomb, and as she wept she stooped to look into the tomb; and she saw two angels in white, sitting where the body of Jesus had lain, one at the head and one at the feet. They said to her, "Woman, why are you weeping?" She said to them, "Because they have taken away my Lord, and I do not know where they have laid him." Saying this, she turned round and saw Jesus standing, but she did not know that it was Jesus. Jesus said to her, "Woman, why are you weeping? Whom do you seek?" Supposing him to be the gardener, she said to him, "Sir, if you have carried him away, tell me where you have laid him, and I will take him away." Jesus said to her, "Mary." She turned and said to him in Hebrew, "Rabboni!" (which means Teacher). Jesus said to her, "Do not hold me, for I have not yet ascended to the Father; but go to my brethren and say to them, I am ascending to my Father and your Father, to my God and your God." Mary Magdalene went and said to the disciples, "I have seen the Lord"; and she told them that he had said these things to her.

Benedictus

Blessed be the Lord, the God of Israel; *
he has come to his people and set them free.
He has raised up for us a mighty Saviour, *
born of the house of his servant David.
Through his holy prophets he promised of old,
that he would save us from our enemies, *
from the hands of all who hate us.
He promised to show mercy to our fathers *
and to remember his holy covenant.
This was the oath he swore
to our father Abraham, *
to set us free from the hands of our enemies,
Free to worship him without fear, *
holy and righteous in his sight
all the days of our life.
You, my child, shall be called the prophet
of the Most High, *
for you will go before the Lord
to prepare his way,
To give his people knowledge of salvation *
by the forgiveness of their sins.
In the tender compassion of our God *
the dawn from on high shall break upon us,
To shine on those who dwell in darkness
and the shadow of death, *
and to guide our feet into the way of peace.

Luke 1.68–79

God of Life, who for our redemption
gave your only-begotten Son
to the death of the cross,
and by his glorious resurrection
have delivered us
from the power of our enemy:
grant us so to die daily to sin,
that we may evermore live with him
in the joy of his risen life;
through Jesus Christ our Lord. Amen.

Our Father in heaven
hallowed be your name,
your kingdom come,
your will be done,
on earth as in heaven.
Give us today our daily bread.
Forgive us our sins
as we forgive those who sin against us.
Lead us not into temptation
but deliver us from evil.
For the kingdom, the power and the glory
are yours now and forever. Amen.

The grace of our Lord Jesus Christ
and the love of God
and the fellowship of the Holy Spirit
be with us all, evermore. Amen.

Sunday Evening

O God make speed to save us.
  O Lord make haste to help us.

Hymn *Crown him with many crowns*

Crown him with many crowns,
    the Lamb upon his throne;
Hark! how the heavenly anthem drowns
    all music but its own:
Awake, my soul, and sing of him
    who died for thee,
And hail him as thy matchless King
    through all eternity.

Crown him the Lord of love!
    Behold his hands and side,
Rich wounds yet visible above
    in beauty glorified:
No angel in the sky
    can fully bear that sight,
But downward bends his burning eye
    at mysteries so bright.

Crown him the Lord of years,
the Potentate of time,
Creator of the rolling spheres,
ineffably sublime.
Glassed in a sea of light,
where everlasting waves
Reflect his throne—the Infinite!
Who lives—and loves—and saves.

Psalm 112 *Beatus vir*

1 Hallelujah!
Happy are they who fear the Lord *
and have great delight in his commandments!
2 Their descendants will be mighty in the land; *
the generation of the upright will be blessed.
3 Wealth and riches will be in their house, *
and their righteousness will last for ever.
4 Light shines in the darkness for the upright; *
the righteous are merciful
and full of compassion.
5 It is good for them to be generous in lending *
and to manage their affairs with justice.
6 For they will never be shaken; *
the righteous will be kept
in everlasting remembrance.

7 They will not be afraid of any evil rumours; *
their heart is right;
they put their trust in the Lord.
8 Their heart is established and will not shrink, *
until they see their desire upon their enemies.
9 They have given freely to the poor, *
and their righteousness stands fast for ever;
they will hold up their head with honour.
10 The wicked will see it and be angry;
they will gnash their teeth and pine away; *
the desires of the wicked will perish.

Psalm 113 *Laudate, pueri*

1 Hallelujah!
Give praise, you servants of the Lord; *
praise the name of the Lord.
2 Let the name of the Lord be blessed, *
from this time forth for evermore.
3 From the rising of the sun to its going down *
let the name of the Lord be praised.
4 The Lord is high above all nations, *
and his glory above the heavens.
5 Who is like the Lord our God,
who sits enthroned on high, *
but stoops to behold the heavens
and the earth?

6 He takes up the weak out of the dust *
   and lifts up the poor from the ashes.
7 He sets them with the princes, *
   with the princes of his people.
8 He makes the woman of a childless house *
   to be a joyful mother of children.

Acts 2.1–4

When the day of Pentecost had come, they were all together in one place. And suddenly a sound came from heaven like the rush of a mighty wind, and it filled all the house where they were sitting. And there appeared to them tongues as of fire, distributed and resting on each one of them. And they were all filled with the Holy Spirit and began to speak in other tongues, as the Spirit gave them utterance.

Matthew 28.16–20

Now the eleven disciples went to Galilee, to the mountain to which Jesus had directed them. And when they saw him they worshipped him; but some doubted. And Jesus came and said to them, "All authority in heaven and on earth has been given to me. Go therefore and make disciples of all nations, baptizing them in the name of the Father and of the Son and of the Holy Spirit, teaching them to observe all that I have commanded you; and lo, I am with you always, to the close of the age."

Magnificat

My soul proclaims the greatness of the Lord,
my spirit rejoices in God my Saviour; *
for he has looked with favour
on his lowly servant.
From this day all generations will call me blessed; *
the Almighty has done great things for me,
and holy is his name.
He has mercy on those who fear him *
in every generation.
He has shown the strength of his arm, *
he has scattered the proud in their conceit.
He has cast down the mighty from their thrones, *
and has lifted up the lowly.
He has filled the hungry with good things, *
and the rich he has sent away empty.
He has come to the help of his servant Israel, *
for he has remembered his promise of mercy,
The promise he made to our fathers, *
to Abraham and his children for ever.

Luke 1.46–55

Almighty God,
by triumphing over the powers of darkness
Christ prepared a place for us
in the new Jerusalem.
May we, who have this day given thanks
for his resurrection, praise him
in the eternal city of which he is the light;
who lives and reigns with you
and the Holy Spirit, one God,
now and for ever. Amen.

Our Father in heaven
hallowed be your name,
your kingdom come,
your will be done,
on earth as in heaven.
Give us today our daily bread.
Forgive us our sins
as we forgive those who sin against us.
Lead us not into temptation
but deliver us from evil.
For the kingdom, the power
and the glory are yours
now and forever. Amen.

To the only God, immortal, invisible,
be glory in the Church and in Christ Jesus,
for ever and ever. Amen.

Monday Morning

O Lord open our lips.
  And our mouth shall proclaim your praise.

Hymn *O praise ye the Lord*

O praise ye the Lord! praise him in the height;
Rejoice in his word, ye angels of light;
Ye heavens adore him by whom ye were made,
And worship before him, in brightness arrayed.

O praise ye the Lord! all things that give sound;
Each jubilant chord, re-echo around;
Loud organs, his glory forth tell in deep tone,
And sweet harp, the story of what he has done.

O praise ye the Lord! thanksgiving and song
To him be outpoured all ages along:
For love in creation, for heaven restored,
For grace of salvation, O praise ye the Lord!

Psalm 121 *Levavi oculos*

1 I lift up my eyes to the hills; *
  from where is my help to come?
2 My help comes from the Lord, *
  the maker of heaven and earth.
3 He will not let your foot be moved *
  and he who watches over you
    will not fall asleep.
4 Behold, he who keeps watch over Israel *
  shall neither slumber nor sleep;
5 The Lord himself watches over you; *
  the Lord is your shade at your right hand,
6 So that the sun shall not strike you by day, *
  nor the moon by night.
7 The Lord shall preserve you from all evil; *
  it is he who shall keep you safe.
8 The Lord shall watch over your going out
    and your coming in, *
  from this time forth for evermore.

Psalm 122 *Lætatus sum*

1 I was glad when they said to me, *
  "Let us go to the house of the Lord."
2 Now our feet are standing *
  within your gates, O Jerusalem.

3 Jerusalem is built as a city *
that is at unity with itself.
4 To which the tribes go up,
the tribes of the Lord, *
the assembly of Israel,
to praise the name of the Lord.
5 For there are the thrones of judgement, *
the thrones of the house of David.
6 Pray for the peace of Jerusalem: *
"May they prosper who love you.
7 Peace be within your walls *
and quietness within your towers.
8 For my brethren and companions' sake, *
I pray for your prosperity.
9 Because of the house of the Lord our God, *
I will seek to do you good."

The Song of the Wilderness

1 The wilderness and the dry land shall rejoice *
the desert shall burst into song;
2 They shall see the glory of the Lord *
the splendour of our God.
3 Strengthen the weary hands *
make firm the feeble knees.
4 Say to the anxious *
"Be strong, fear not!

5 Your God is coming with judgement *
coming with judgement to save you."

Isaiah 35.1–4

John 1.1–9

In the beginning was the Word, and the Word was with God, and the Word was God. He was in the beginning with God; all things were made through him, and without him was not anything made that was made. In him was life, and the life was the light of men. The light shines in the darkness, and the darkness has not overcome it. There was a man sent from God, whose name was John. He came for testimony, to bear witness to the light, that all might believe through him. He was not the light, but came to bear witness to the light. The true light that enlightens every man was coming into the world.

Luke 1.26–38

In the sixth month the angel Gabriel was sent from God to a city of Galilee named Nazareth, to a virgin betrothed to a man whose name was Joseph, of the house of David; and the virgin's name was Mary. And he came to her and said, "Hail, O favoured one, the Lord is with you!" But she was greatly troubled at the saying, and considered in her mind what sort of greeting this might be. And the angel said to her,

"Do not be afraid, Mary, for you have found favour with God. And behold, you will conceive in your womb and bear a son, and you shall call his name Jesus. He will be great, and will be called the Son of the Most High; and the Lord God will give to him the throne of his father David, and he will reign over the house of Jacob for ever; and of his kingdom there will be no end." And Mary said to the angel, "How shall this be, since I have no husband?" And the angel said to her, "The Holy Spirit will come upon you, and the power of the Most High will overshadow you; therefore the child to be born will be called holy, the Son of God. And behold, your kinswoman Elizabeth in her old age has also conceived a son; and this is the sixth month with her who was called barren. For with God nothing will be impossible." And Mary said, "Behold, I am the handmaid of the Lord; let it be to me according to your word." And the angel departed from her.

Almighty and everlasting Father,
we thank you that you have brought us
safely to the beginning of this day.
Keep us from falling into sin
or running into danger;
order us in all our doings;
and guide us to do always
what is right in your eyes;
through Jesus Christ our Lord. Amen.

Our Father…

The grace of our Lord Jesus Christ
and the love of God
and the fellowship of the Holy Spirit
be with us all, evermore. Amen.

Monday Evening

O God make speed to save us.
  O Lord make haste to help us.

Hymn *At the name of Jesus*

At the name of Jesus, every knee shall bow,
Every tongue confess him King of glory now;
'Tis the Father's pleasure we should call him Lord,
Who from the beginning was the mighty Word.

At his voice creation sprang at once to sight,
All the angel faces, all the hosts of light,
Thrones and dominations, stars upon their way,
All the heavenly orders, in their great array.

Humbled for a season, to receive a name
From the lips of sinners unto whom he came,
Faithfully he bore it, spotless to the last,
Brought it back victorious
    when from death he passed.

In your hearts enthrone him;
there let him subdue
All that is not holy, all that is not true:
He is God the Saviour, he is Christ the Lord,
Ever to be worshipped, trusted and adored.

Psalm 62 *Nonne Deo?*

1 For God alone my soul in silence waits; *
from him comes my salvation.
2 He alone is my rock and my salvation, *
my stronghold, so that I shall not be
greatly shaken.
3 How long will you assail me to crush me,
all of you together, *
as if you were a leaning fence,
a toppling wall?
4 They seek only to bring me down
from my place of honour; *
lies are their chief delight.
5 They bless with their lips, *
but in their hearts they curse.
6 For God alone my soul in silence waits; *
truly, my hope is in him.
7 He alone is my rock and my salvation, *
my stronghold, so that I shall not be shaken.

8 In God is my safety and my honour; ⋆
God is my strong rock and my refuge.

9 Put your trust in him always, O people, ⋆
pour out your hearts before him,
for God is our refuge.

10 Those of high degree are but a fleeting breath, ⋆
even those of low estate cannot be trusted.

11 On the scales they are lighter than a breath, ⋆
all of them together.

12 Put no trust in extortion;
in robbery take no empty pride; ⋆
though wealth increase,
set not your heart upon it.

13 God has spoken once, twice have I heard it, ⋆
that power belongs to God.

14 Steadfast love is yours, O Lord, ⋆
for you repay everyone according to his deeds.

A Song of Redemption

1 Blessed be the God and Father
of our Lord Jesus Christ ⋆
who has blessed us in Christ
with every spiritual blessing
in the heavenly places.

2 He chose us in him before the foundation
of the world ⋆

that we should be holy and blameless
before him.

3 He predestined us in love *
to be adopted as his children
through Jesus Christ.

4 According to the purpose of his will,
to the praise of his glorious grace *
which he freely bestowed on us
in the Beloved.

5 In him we have redemption
through his blood,
the forgiveness of our trespasses, *
according to the riches of his grace,
which he lavished upon us.

6 He has made known to us,
in all wisdom and insight, *
the mystery of his will
according to his purpose
which he set forth in Christ.

7 A plan for the fullness of time,
to unite all things in him *
things in heaven and things on earth.

Ephesians 1.3–10

Matthew 3.13–17

Then Jesus came from Galilee to the Jordan to John, to be baptized by him. John would have prevented him, saying, "I need to be baptized by you, and do you come to me?" But Jesus answered him, "Let it be so now; for thus it is fitting for us to fulfil all righteousness." Then he consented. And when Jesus was baptized, he went up immediately from the water, and behold, the heavens were opened and he saw the Spirit of God descending like a dove, and alighting on him; and lo, a voice from heaven, saying, "This is my beloved Son, with whom I am well pleased."

Luke 2.25-35

Now there was a man in Jerusalem, whose name was Simeon, and this man was righteous and devout, looking for the consolation of Israel, and the Holy Spirit was upon him. And it had been revealed to him by the Holy Spirit that he should not see death before he had seen the Lord's Christ. And inspired by the Spirit he came into the temple; and when the parents brought in the child Jesus, to do for him according to the custom of the law, he took him up in his arms and blessed God and said, "Lord, now lettest thou thy servant depart in peace, according to thy word; for mine eyes have seen thy salvation which thou hast prepared in the presence of all peoples, a light for revelation to the Gentiles, and for glory to thy people Israel." And his father and his mother marvelled at what was said about him; and Simeon blessed them and said to Mary his mother, "Behold, this child is set for the fall and rising of many in Israel, and for a sign that is spoken against (and a sword will pierce through your own soul also), that thoughts out of many hearts may be revealed."

Lighten our darkness, Lord we pray;
and in your mercy defend us
from all perils and dangers of this night;
for the love of your only Son,
our Saviour Jesus Christ. Amen.

Our Father...

To the only God, immortal, invisible,
be glory in the Church and in Christ Jesus,
for ever and ever. Amen.

Tuesday Morning

O Lord open our lips.
  And our mouth shall proclaim your praise.

Hymn *Dear Lord and Father of mankind*

Dear Lord and Father of mankind,
Forgive our foolish ways!
Re-clothe us in our rightful mind,
In purer lives thy service find,
In deeper reverence praise.

Drop thy still dews of quietness,
Till all our strivings cease;
Take from our souls the strain and stress,
And let our ordered lives confess
The beauty of thy peace.

Breathe through the heats of our desire
Thy coolness and thy balm;
Let sense be dumb, let flesh retire;
Speak through the earthquake, wind, and fire,
O still small voice of calm.

Psalm 70 *Deus in adjutorium*

1 Be pleased, O God, to deliver me; *
O Lord, make haste to help me.

2 Let those who seek my life be ashamed
and altogether dismayed; *
let those who take pleasure in my misfortune
draw back and be disgraced.

3 Let those who say to me "Aha!"
and gloat over me turn back, *
because they are ashamed.

4 Let all who seek you rejoice and be glad in you; *
let those who love your salvation say for ever,
"Great is the Lord!"

5 But as for me, I am poor and needy; *
come to me speedily, O God.

6 You are my helper and my deliverer; *
O Lord, do not tarry.

The Souls of the Righteous

1 The souls of the righteous
are in the hand of God *
and no torment will touch them.

2 In the eyes of the foolish they seemed to have died *
and their departure
was thought to be an affliction,

3 And their going from us
to be their destruction *
but they are at peace.
4 For though in the sight of men
they were punished *
their hope is full of immortality.
5 Having been disciplined a little,
they will receive great good *
because God tested them
and found them worthy of himself.
6 Like gold in the furnace he tried them *
and like a burnt offering he accepted them.
7 In the time of his visitation they will shine forth *
and will run like sparks through the stubble.
8 They will govern nations and rule over peoples *
and the Lord will reign over them for ever.
9 Those who trust in him will understand truth *
and the faithful will abide with him in love.
10 Because grace and mercy are upon his elect *
and he watches over his holy ones.

Wisdom 3.1–9

Mark 1.16-20

And passing along by the Sea of Galilee, he saw Simon and Andrew the brother of Simon casting a net in the sea; for they were fishermen. And Jesus said to them, "Follow me and I will make you become fishers of men." And immediately they left their nets and followed him. And going on a little farther, he saw James the son of Zebedee and John his brother, who were in their boat mending the nets. And immediately he called them; and they left their father Zebedee in the boat with the hired servants, and followed him.

Matthew 4.1-11

Then Jesus was led up by the Spirit into the wilderness to be tempted by the devil. And he fasted forty days and forty nights, and afterward he was hungry. And the tempter came and said to him, "If you are the Son of God, command these stones to become loaves of bread." But he answered, "It is written, 'Man shall not live by bread alone, but by every word that proceeds from the mouth of God.'" Then the devil took him to the holy city, and set him on the pinnacle of the temple, and said to him, "If you are the Son of God, throw yourself down; for it is written, 'He will give his angels charge of you,' and 'On their hands they will bear you up, lest you strike your foot against a stone.'" Jesus said to him, "Again it is written, 'You shall not tempt the Lord your God.'" Again, the devil took him to a very high mountain, and showed him all the kingdoms of the world and the glory of them; and he said to him, "All these I will give you, if you will fall down and worship me." Then Jesus said to him, "Begone, Satan! for it is written, 'You shall worship the Lord your God and him only shall you serve.'" Then the devil left him, and behold, angels came and ministered to him.

Almighty and everlasting God,
by whose Spirit the whole body of the Church
is governed and sanctified:
hear our prayer which we offer
for all your faithful people;
that each in their vocation and ministry
may serve you in holiness
and truth to the glory of your name;
through our Lord and Saviour Jesus Christ.
Amen.

Our Father...

The grace of our Lord Jesus Christ
and the love of God
and the fellowship of the Holy Spirit
be with us all, evermore. Amen.

Tuesday Evening

O God make speed to save us.
O Lord make haste to help us.

Hymn *Praise to the Lord, the Almighty*

Praise to the Lord, the Almighty,
the King of creation;
O my soul, praise him,
for he is thy health and salvation:
Come ye who hear, brothers and sisters draw near;
Praise him in glad adoration.

Praise to the Lord, who o'er all things
so wondrously reigneth,
Shelters thee under his wings,
yea, so gently sustaineth:
Hast thou not seen all that is needful hath been
Granted in what he ordaineth?

Praise to the Lord!
O let all that is in me adore him!
All that hath life and breath
come now with praises before him!
Let the Amen sound from his people again:
Gladly for all we adore him.

Psalm 19 *Cæli enarrant*

1 The heavens declare the glory of God, *
  and the firmament shows his handiwork.
2 One day tells its tale to another, *
  and one night imparts knowledge to another.
3 Although they have no words or language, *
  and their voices are not heard,
4 Their sound has gone out into all lands, *
  and their message to the ends of the world.
5 In the deep has he set a pavilion for the sun; *
  it comes forth like a bridegroom
    out of his chamber;
    it rejoices like a champion to run its course.
6 It goes forth from the uttermost edge
    of the heavens and runs about
    to the end of it again; *
  nothing is hidden from its burning heat.
7 The law of the Lord is perfect
    and revives the soul; *
  the testimony of the Lord is sure
    and gives wisdom to the innocent.
8 The statutes of the Lord are just
    and rejoice the heart; *
  the commandment of the Lord is clear
    and gives light to the eyes.
9 The fear of the Lord is clean
    and endures for ever; *

the judgements of the Lord are true
and righteous altogether.

10 More to be desired are they than gold,
more than much fine gold, *
sweeter far than honey,
than honey in the comb.

11 By them also is your servant enlightened, *
and in keeping them there is great reward.

12 Who can tell how often he offends? *
Cleanse me from my secret faults.

13 Above all, keep your servant
from presumptuous sins;
let them not get dominion over me; *
then shall I be whole and sound,
and innocent of a great offence.

14 Let the words of my mouth and the meditation
of my heart be acceptable in your sight, *
O Lord, my strength and my redeemer.

The Beatitudes

1 Blessed are the poor in spirit *
for theirs is the kingdom of heaven.

2 Blessed are those who mourn, *
for they shall be comforted.

3 Blessed are the meek, *
for they shall inherit the earth.

4 Blessed are those who hunger and thirst
for righteousness, *
for they shall be satisfied.
5 Blessed are the merciful, *
for they shall obtain mercy.
6 Blessed are the pure in heart, *
for they shall see God.
7 Blessed are the peacemakers, *
for they shall be called sons of God.
8 Blessed are those who are persecuted
on account of righteousness, *
for theirs is the kingdom of heaven.

Matthew 5.3–10

Luke 4.16–21

And he came to Nazareth, where he had been brought up; and he went to the synagogue, as his custom was, on the sabbath day. And he stood up to read; and there was given to him the book of the prophet Isaiah. He opened the book and found the place where it was written, "The Spirit of the Lord is upon me, because he has anointed me to preach good news to the poor. He has sent me to proclaim release to the captives and recovering of sight to the blind, to set at liberty those who are oppressed, to proclaim the acceptable year of the Lord." And he closed the book, and gave it back to the attendant, and sat down; and the eyes of all in the synagogue were fixed on him. And he began to say to them, "Today this scripture has been fulfilled in your hearing."

John 9.1–8

As he passed by, he saw a man blind from his birth. And his disciples asked him, "Rabbi, who sinned, this man or his parents, that he was born blind?" Jesus answered, "It was not that this man sinned, or his parents, but that the works of God might be made manifest in him. We must work the works of him who sent me, while it is day; night comes, when no one can work. As long as I am in the world, I am the light of the world." As he said this, he spat on the ground and made clay of the spittle and anointed the man's eyes with the clay, saying to him, "Go, wash in the pool of Siloam" (which means Sent). So he went and washed and came back seeing. The neighbours and those who had seen him before as a beggar, said, "Is not this the man who used to sit and beg?"

Be present, O merciful God, and protect us
through the silent hours of this night
so that we who are wearied
by the changes and chances
of this fleeting world
may rest in your eternal changelessness;
through Jesus Christ our Lord. Amen.

Our Father…

To the only God, immortal, invisible,
be glory in the Church and in Christ Jesus,
for ever and ever. Amen.

Wednesday Morning

O Lord open our lips.
  And our mouth shall proclaim your praise.

Hymn *Be thou my vision*

Be thou my vision, O Lord of my heart;
Be all else but naught to me, save that thou art,
Be thou my best thought, in the day and the night,
Both waking and sleeping, thy presence my light.

Be thou my wisdom, be thou my true word
Be thou ever with me, and I with thee, Lord,
Be thou my great Father, and I thy true son;
Be thou in me dwelling, and I with thee one.

High King of heaven, thou heaven's bright Sun,
O grant me its joys after victory is won,
Great heart of my own heart, whatever befall,
Still be thou my vision, O Ruler of all.

Psalm 126 *In convertendo*

1 When the Lord restored the fortunes of Zion, *
then were we like those who dream.
2 Then was our mouth filled with laughter, *
and our tongue with shouts of joy.
3 Then they said among the nations, *
"The Lord has done great things for them."
4 The Lord has done great things for us, *
and we are glad indeed.
5 Restore our fortunes, O Lord, *
like the watercourses of the Negev.
6 Those who sowed with tears *
will reap with songs of joy.
7 Those who go out weeping, carrying the seed, *
will come again with joy,
shouldering their sheaves.

Psalm 127 *Nisi Dominus*

1 Unless the Lord builds the house, *
their labour is in vain who build it.
2 Unless the Lord watches over the city, *
in vain the watchman keeps his vigil.
3 It is in vain that you rise so early
and go to bed so late; *
vain, too, to eat the bread of toil,
for he gives to his beloved sleep.

4 Children are a heritage from the Lord, ⋆
 and the fruit of the womb is a gift.
5 Like arrows in the hand of a warrior ⋆
 are the children of one's youth.
6 Happy is the man
  who has his quiver full of them! ⋆
 he shall not be put to shame when
  he contends with his enemies in the gate.

A Song of Good News

1 Go up to a high mountain, ⋆
 O Zion, herald of joy;
2 Lift up your voice in strength, ⋆
 Jerusalem, herald of joy;
3 Lift it up, fear not; ⋆
 say to the cities of Judah: "Behold your God!
4 Behold, the Lord comes in might, ⋆
 comes to rule with his mighty arm;
5 Behold, his reward is with him, ⋆
 his recompense before him.
6 Like a shepherd will he feed his flock, ⋆
 gathering the lambs in his arms;
7 He will hold them to his breast ⋆
 and gently lead those with young."

Isaiah 40.9–11

Mark 10.17–22

And as he was setting out on his journey, a man ran up and knelt before him, and asked him, "Good Teacher, what must I do to inherit eternal life?" And Jesus said to him, "Why do you call me good? No one is good but God alone. You know the commandments: 'Do not kill, Do not commit adultery, Do not steal, Do not bear false witness, Do not defraud, Honour your father and mother.'" And he said to him, "Teacher, all these I have observed from my youth." And Jesus looking upon him loved him, and said to him, "You lack one thing; go, sell what you have, and give to the poor, and you will have treasure in heaven; and come, follow me." At that saying his countenance fell, and he went away sorrowful; for he had great possessions.

Luke 10.30–37

Jesus replied, "A man was going down from Jerusalem to Jericho, and he fell among robbers, who stripped him and beat him, and departed, leaving him half dead. Now by chance a priest was going down that road; and when he saw him he passed by on the other side. So likewise a Levite, when he came to the place and saw him, passed by on the other side. But a Samaritan, as he journeyed, came to where he was; and when he saw him, he had compassion, and went to him and bound up his wounds, pouring on oil and wine; then he set him on his own beast and brought him to an inn, and took care of him. And the next day he took out two denarii and gave them to the innkeeper, saying, 'Take care of him; and whatever more you spend, I will repay you when I come back.' Which of these three, do you think, proved neighbour to the man who fell among the robbers?" He said, "The one who showed mercy on him." And Jesus said to him, "Go and do likewise."

Eternal God and Father,
you create us by your power
and redeem us by your love:
guide and strengthen us by your Spirit,
that we may give ourselves in love and service
to one another and to you;
through Jesus Christ our Lord. Amen.

Our Father...

The grace of our Lord Jesus Christ
and the love of God
and the fellowship of the Holy Spirit
be with us all, evermore. Amen.

Wednesday Evening

O God make speed to save us.
  O Lord make haste to help us.

Hymn *Lead, kindly Light*

Lead, kindly Light, amid the encircling gloom,
    lead thou me on;
The night is dark, and I am far from home,
    lead thou me on.
Keep thou my feet; I do not ask to see
The distant scene; one step enough for me.

I was not ever thus, nor prayed that thou
    shouldst lead me on;
I loved to choose and see my path; but now
    lead thou me on.
I loved the garish day, and, spite of fears,
Pride ruled my will: remember not past years.

So long thy power hath blest me, sure it still
    will lead me on
O'er moor and fen, o'er crag and torrent,
    till the night is gone,
And with the morn those angel faces smile,
Which I have loved long since, and lost awhile.

Psalm 24 *Domini est terra*

1 The earth is the Lord's and all that is in it, *
the world and all who dwell therein.

2 For it is he who founded it upon the seas *
and made it firm upon the rivers of the deep.

3 "Who can ascend the hill of the Lord? *
and who can stand in his holy place?"

4 "Those who have clean hands and a pure heart, *
who have not pledged themselves to falsehood,
nor sworn by what is a fraud.

5 They shall receive a blessing from the Lord *
and a just reward from the God
of their salvation."

6 Such is the generation of those who seek him, *
of those who seek your face, O God of Jacob.

7 Lift up your heads, O gates;
lift them high, O everlasting doors; *
and the King of glory shall come in.

8 "Who is this King of glory?" *
"The Lord, strong and mighty,
the Lord, mighty in battle."

9 Lift up your heads, O gates;
lift them high, O everlasting doors; *
and the King of glory shall come in.

10 "Who is he, this King of glory?" *
"The Lord of hosts, he is the King of glory."

Psalm 128 *Beati omnes*

1 Happy are they all who fear the Lord, *
  and who follow in his ways!
2 You shall eat the fruit of your labour; *
  happiness and prosperity shall be yours.
3 Your wife shall be like a fruitful vine
    within your house, *
  your children like olive shoots
    round about your table.
4 The man who fears the Lord *
  shall thus indeed be blessed.
5 The Lord bless you from Zion, *
  and may you see the prosperity of Jerusalem
    all the days of your life.
6 May you live to see your children's children; *
  may peace be upon Israel.

A Song from Ezekiel

1 I will take you from the nations,
    and gather you from every country, *
  and bring you home to your own land.
2 I will pour clean water upon you,
    purify you from all defilement, *
    and cleanse you from all your idols.

3 A new heart I will give you,
and put a new spirit within you; *
I will take from your body the heart of stone
and give you a heart of flesh.
4 I will put my spirit within you, *
make you walk in my ways
and observe my decrees.
5 You shall dwell in the land
I gave to your forebears; *
you shall be my people
and I will be your God.

Ezekiel 36.24–28

Luke 18.9–14

He also told this parable to some who trusted in themselves that they were righteous and despised others: "Two men went up into the temple to pray, one a Pharisee and the other a tax collector. The Pharisee stood and prayed thus with himself, 'God, I thank thee that I am not like other men, extortioners, unjust, adulterers, or even like this tax collector. I fast twice a week, I give tithes of all that I get.' But the tax collector, standing far off, would not even lift up his eyes to heaven, but beat his breast, saying, 'God, be merciful to me a sinner!' I tell you, this man went down to his house justified rather than the other; for every one who exalts himself will be humbled, but he who humbles himself will be exalted."

Mark 10.46–52

And they came to Jericho; and as he was leaving Jericho with his disciples and a great multitude, Bartimaeus, a blind beggar, the son of Timaeus, was sitting by the roadside. And when he heard that it was Jesus of Nazareth, he began to cry out and say, "Jesus, Son of David, have mercy on me!" And many rebuked him, telling him to be silent; but he cried out all the more, "Son of David, have mercy on me!" And Jesus stopped and said, "Call him." And they called the blind man, saying to him, "Take heart; rise, he is calling you." And throwing off his mantle he sprang up and came to Jesus. And Jesus said to him, "What do you want me to do for you?" And the blind man said to him, "Master, let me receive my sight." And Jesus said to him, "Go your way; your faith has made you well." And immediately he received his sight and followed him on the way.

Look down, O Lord,
from your heavenly throne,
illuminate the darkness of this night
with your celestial brightness,
and from the children of light
banish the deeds of darkness;
through Jesus Christ our Lord. Amen.

Our Father…

To the only God, immortal, invisible,
be glory in the Church and in Christ Jesus,
for ever and ever. Amen.

Thursday Morning

O Lord open our lips.
  And our mouth shall proclaim your praise.

Hymn *Guide me, O thou great Redeemer*

Guide me, O thou great Redeemer,
Pilgrim through this barren land;
I am weak, but thou art mighty,
Hold me with thy powerful hand:
  Bread of heaven,
  Feed me till I want no more.

Open now the crystal fountain
Where the living stream doth flow;
Let the fire and cloudy pillar
Lead me all my journey through:
  Strong Deliverer,
  Be thou still my strength and shield.

When I tread the verge of Jordan,
Bid my anxious fears subside;
Death of death and hell's Destruction,
Land me safe on Canaan's side:
  Songs of praises
  I will ever give to thee.

Psalm 135 *Laudate nomen*

1 Hallelujah!
Praise the name of the Lord; *
give praise, you servants of the Lord,
2 You who stand in the house of the Lord, *
in the courts of the house of our God.
3 Praise the Lord, for the Lord is good; *
sing praises to his name, for it is lovely.
4 For the Lord has chosen Jacob for himself *
and Israel for his own possession.
5 For I know that the Lord is great, *
and that our Lord is above all gods.
6 The Lord does whatever pleases him,
in heaven and on earth, *
in the seas and all the deeps.
7 He brings up rain clouds
from the ends of the earth; *
he sends out lightning with the rain,
and brings the winds out of his storehouse.
8 It was he who struck down
the first-born of Egypt, *
the first-born both of human and beast.
9 He sent signs and wonders
into the midst of you, O Egypt, *
against Pharaoh and all his servants.
10 He overthrew many nations *
and put mighty kings to death:

11 Sihon, king of the Amorites,
and Og, the king of Bashan, *
and all the kingdoms of Canaan.
12 He gave their land to be an inheritance, *
an inheritance for Israel his people.
13 O Lord, your name is everlasting; *
your renown, O Lord, endures from age to age.
14 For the Lord gives his people justice *
and shows compassion to his servants.
15 The idols of the heathen are silver and gold, *
the work of human hands.
16 They have mouths, but they cannot speak; *
eyes have they, but they cannot see.
17 They have ears, but they cannot hear; *
neither is there any breath in their mouth.
18 Those who make them are like them, *
and so are all who put their trust in them.
19 Bless the Lord, O house of Israel; *
O house of Aaron, bless the Lord.
20 Bless the Lord, O house of Levi; *
you who fear the Lord, bless the Lord.
21 Blessed be the Lord out of Zion, *
who dwells in Jerusalem. Hallelujah!

A Song of Salvation

1 Praise be to the God and Father
  of our Lord Jesus Christ,
  who in his great mercy
  gave us a new birth into a living hope *
 by the resurrection of Jesus Christ from the dead.

2 The inheritance to which we were born
  is one that nothing can destroy
  or spoil or wither; *
 it is kept for you in heaven.

3 And you, because you put your faith in God *
 are under the protection of his power
  until salvation comes;

4 The salvation which is even now in readiness *
 and will be revealed at the end of time.

5 God raised him up from the dead
  and gave him glory *
 that your faith and hope might be in God.

1 Peter 1.3,4,21

John 6.53–58

So Jesus said to them, "Truly, truly, I say to you, unless you eat the flesh of the Son of man and drink his blood, you have no life in you; he who eats my flesh and drinks my blood has eternal life, and I will raise him up at the last day. For my flesh is food indeed, and my blood is drink indeed. He who eats my flesh and drinks my blood abides in me, and I in him. As the living Father sent me, and I live because of the Father, so he who eats me will live because of me. This is the bread which came down from heaven, not such as the fathers ate and died; he who eats this bread will live for ever."

Mark 6.35–42

And when it grew late, his disciples came to him and said, "This is a lonely place, and the hour is now late; send them away, to go into the country and villages round about and buy themselves something to eat." But he answered them, "You give them something to eat." And they said to him, "Shall we go and buy two hundred denarii worth of bread, and give it to them to eat?" And he said to them, "How many loaves have you? Go and see." And when they had found out, they said, "Five, and two fish." Then he commanded them all to sit down by companies upon the green grass. So they sat down in groups, by hundreds and by fifties. And taking the five loaves and the two fish he looked up to heaven, and blessed, and broke the loaves, and gave them to the disciples to set before the people; and he divided the two fish among them all. And they all ate and were satisfied.

O Christ,
whose heart was moved with compassion
for the hunger of the multitude,
and who used your disciples
to minister to their needs:
fill us with your own love and concern
for the hungry peoples of the world,
and make us the instruments of your purpose
to relieve their sufferings;
for your tender mercy's sake. Amen.

Our Father…

The grace of our Lord Jesus Christ
and the love of God
and the fellowship of the Holy Spirit
be with us all, evermore. Amen.

Thursday Evening

O God make speed to save us.
  O Lord make haste to help us.

Hymn *Alleluya, sing to Jesus*

Alleluya, sing to Jesus,
  his the sceptre, his the throne;
Alleluya, his the triumph,
  his the victory alone:
Hark the songs of peaceful Sion
  thunder like a mighty flood;
Jesus, out of every nation,
  hath redeemed us by his blood.

Alleluya, King eternal,
  thee the Lord of lords we own;
Alleluya, born of Mary,
  earth thy footstool, heaven thy throne:
Thou within the veil hast entered,
  robed in flesh, our great High Priest;
Thou on earth both Priest and Victim
  in the Eucharistic feast.

Psalm 89 *Misericordias Domini*

1 Your love, O Lord, for ever will I sing; *
from age to age my mouth
will proclaim your faithfulness.
2 For I am persuaded that your love
is established for ever; *
you have set your faithfulness
firmly in the heavens.
3 'I have made a covenant with my chosen one; *
I have sworn an oath to David my servant:
4 "I will establish your line for ever, *
and preserve your throne for all generations."'
5 The heavens bear witness
to your wonders, O Lord, *
and to your faithfulness
in the assembly of the holy ones;
6 For who in the skies can be compared
to the Lord? *
who is like the Lord among the gods?
7 God is much to be feared
in the council of the holy ones, *
great and terrible to all those round about him.
8 Who is like you, Lord God of hosts? *
O mighty Lord, your faithfulness
is all around you.

9 You rule the raging of the sea *
and still the surging of its waves.

10 You have crushed Rahab of the deep
with a deadly wound; *
you have scattered your enemies
with your mighty arm.

11 Yours are the heavens; the earth also is yours; *
you laid the foundations of the world
and all that is in it.

12 You have made the north and the south; *
Tabor and Hermon rejoice in your name.

13 You have a mighty arm; *
strong is your hand and high is your right hand.

14 Righteousness and justice
are the foundations of your throne; *
love and truth go before your face.

15 Happy are the people who know the festal shout! *
they walk, O Lord, in the light of your presence.

16 They rejoice daily in your name; *
they are jubilant in your righteousness.

17 For you are the glory of their strength, *
and by your favour our might is exalted.

18 Truly, the Lord is our ruler; *
the Holy One of Israel is our king.

A Song of Judgement

1 We give thanks to you, Lord God Almighty,
ever present and eternal *
for you have taken your great power
and begun to reign.

2 The nations raged,
but the day of your wrath has come *
and the time for the dead to be judged.

3 The time has come to reward your servants *
the prophets and saints; and those who fear
your name, both small and great.

4 Now the salvation of God has come,
his power and his glorious kingdom; *
now has come the authority of his Christ.

5 For the accuser of our brothers
has been thrown down *
who accuses them day and night before our God.

6 And they have conquered him
by the blood of the Lamb,
and by their word of witness. *
Rejoice then, O heaven,
and you that dwell therein.

Revelation 11.17,18; 12.10–12

John 14.25–29

"These things I have spoken to you, while I am still with you. But the Counsellor, the Holy Spirit, whom the Father will send in my name, he will teach you all things, and bring to your remembrance all that I have said to you. Peace I leave with you; my peace I give to you; not as the world gives do I give to you. Let not your hearts be troubled, neither let them be afraid. You heard me say to you, 'I go away, and I will come to you.' If you loved me, you would have rejoiced, because I go to the Father; for the Father is greater than I. And now I have told you before it takes place, so that when it does take place, you may believe."

Luke 22.14–20

And when the hour came, he sat at table, and the apostles with him. And he said to them, "I have earnestly desired to eat this passover with you before I suffer; for I tell you I shall not eat it until it is fulfilled in the kingdom of God." And he took a cup, and when he had given thanks he said, "Take this, and divide it among yourselves; for I tell you that from now on I shall not drink of the fruit of the vine until the kingdom of God comes." And he took bread, and when he had given thanks he broke it and gave it to them, saying, "This is my body which is given for you. Do this in remembrance of me."

And likewise the cup after supper, saying, "This cup which is poured out for you is the new covenant in my blood."

O God, the Father of our Lord Jesus Christ,
our only Saviour, the Prince of Peace:
give us grace seriously to lay to heart
all the great dangers we are in
by our unhappy divisions.
Take away all hatred and prejudice,
and whatsoever may hinder us
from godly union and concord;
that as there is but one body and one Spirit,
and one hope of our calling, one Lord,
one faith, one baptism, one God and Father
of us all, so we may all be of one heart
and one soul, united in one holy bond
of truth and peace, of faith and charity,
and may with one mind and one mouth
ever proclaim your glory;
through Jesus Christ our Lord. Amen.

Our Father...

To the only God, immortal, invisible,
be glory in the Church and in Christ Jesus,
for ever and ever. Amen.

Friday Morning

O Lord open our lips.
  And our mouth shall proclaim your praise.

Hymn *When morning gilds the skies*

When morning gilds the skies,
My heart awaking cries,
  May Jesus Christ be praised:
Alike at work and prayer
To Jesus I repair;
  May Jesus Christ be praised.

The night becomes as day,
When from the heart we say:
  May Jesus Christ be praised:
The powers of darkness fear,
When this sweet chant they hear,
  May Jesus Christ be praised.

Be this, while life is mine,
My canticle divine,
  May Jesus Christ be praised:
Be this the eternal song
Through all the ages on,
  May Jesus Christ be praised.

Psalm 22 *Deus, Deus meus*

1 My God, my God, why have you forsaken me? *
and are so far from my cry
and from the words of my distress?
2 O my God, I cry in the daytime,
but you do not answer; *
by night as well, but I find no rest.
3 Yet you are the Holy One, *
enthroned upon the praises of Israel.
4 Our forebears put their trust in you; *
they trusted and you delivered them.
5 They cried out to you and were delivered; *
they trusted in you and were not put to shame.
6 But as for me, I am a worm and no man, *
scorned by all and despised by the people.
7 All who see me laugh me to scorn; *
they curl their lips and wag their heads, saying,
8 "He trusted in the Lord; let him deliver him; *
let him rescue him, if he delights in him."
9 Yet you are he who took me out of the womb, *
and kept me safe upon my mother's breast.
10 I have been entrusted to you
ever since I was born; *
you were my God
when I was still in my mother's womb.
11 Be not far from me, for trouble is near, *
and there is none to help.

12 Many young bulls encircle me; *
strong bulls of Bashan surround me.

13 They open wide their jaws at me, *
like a ravening and a roaring lion.

14 I am poured out like water;
all my bones are out of joint; *
my heart within my breast is melting wax.

15 My mouth is dried out like a pot-sherd;
my tongue sticks to the roof of my mouth; *
and you have laid me in the dust of the grave.

16 Packs of dogs close me in,
and gangs of evildoers circle around me; *
they pierce my hands and my feet;
I can count all my bones.

17 They stare and gloat over me; *
they divide my garments among them;
they cast lots for my clothing.

18 Be not far away, O Lord; *
you are my strength; hasten to help me.

19 Save me from the sword, *
my life from the power of the dog.

20 Save me from the lion's mouth, *
my wretched body from the horns of wild bulls.

21 I will declare your name to my people; *
in the midst of the congregation I will praise you.

A Song of Ransom

1 Glory and honour and power *
  are yours by right, O Lord our God.
2 For you created all things, *
  and by your will they have their being.
3 Glory and honour and power, *
  are yours by right, O Lamb who was slain.
4 For by your blood you ransomed for God
    saints from every tribe and language
    and people and nation; *
  to make them worthy to be a kingdom
    and priests to stand and serve before our God.
5 To him who sits on the throne and to the Lamb *
  be praise and honour and might
    for ever and ever. Amen.

Revelation 4.11; 5.12,9,10,13

Luke 9.18–22

Now it happened that as he was praying alone the disciples were with him; and he asked them, "Who do the people say that I am?" And they answered, "John the Baptist; but others say, Elijah; and others, that one of the old prophets has risen." And he said to them, "But who do you say that I am?" And Peter answered, "The Christ of God." But he charged and commanded them to tell this to no one, saying, "The Son of man must suffer many things, and be rejected by the elders and chief priests and scribes, and be killed, and on the third day be raised."

John 12.27–36

"Now is my soul troubled. And what shall I say? 'Father, save me from this hour'? No, for this purpose I have come to this hour. Father, glorify thy name." Then a voice came from heaven, "I have glorified it, and I will glorify it again." The crowd standing by heard it and said that it had thundered. Others said, "An angel has spoken to him." Jesus answered, "This voice has come for your sake, not for mine. Now is the judgement of this world, now shall the ruler of this world be cast out; and I, when I am lifted up from the earth, will draw all men to myself." He said this to show by what death he was to die. The crowd answered him, "We have heard from the law that the Christ remains for ever. How can you say that the Son of man must be lifted up? Who is this Son of man?" Jesus said to them, "The light is with you for a little longer. Walk while you have the light, lest the darkness overtake you; he who walks in the darkness does not know where he goes. While you have the light, believe in the light, that you may become sons of light." When Jesus had said this, he departed and hid himself from them.

Almighty Father,
look with mercy on this your family
for which our Lord Jesus Christ
was content to be betrayed
and given up into the hands of sinners
and to suffer death upon the cross;
who lives and reigns
with you and the Holy Spirit,
one God, now and for ever. Amen.

Our Father…

The grace of our Lord Jesus Christ
and the love of God
and the fellowship of the Holy Spirit
be with us all, evermore. Amen.

Friday Evening

O God make speed to save us.
  O Lord make haste to help us.

Hymn *Just as I am*

Just as I am, without one plea
But that thy blood was shed for me,
And that thou bidst me come to thee,
  O Lamb of God, I come.

Just as I am, poor, wretched, blind;
Sight, riches, healing of the mind,
Yea, all I need, in thee to find,
  O Lamb of God, I come.

Just as I am, thou wilt receive,
Wilt welcome, pardon, cleanse, relieve:
Because thy promise I believe,
  O Lamb of God, I come.

Just as I am (thy love unknown
Has broken every barrier down),
Now to be thine, yea thine alone,
  O Lamb of God, I come.

Just as I am, of that free love
The breadth, length, depth and height to prove,
Here for a season then above,
O Lamb of God, I come.

Psalm 11 *In Domino confido*

1 In the Lord have I taken refuge; *
how then can you say to me,
"Fly away like a bird to the hilltop;
2 For see how the wicked bend the bow
and fit their arrows to the string, *
to shoot from ambush at the true of heart.
3 When the foundations are being destroyed, *
what can the righteous do?"
4 The Lord is in his holy temple; *
the Lord's throne is in heaven.
5 His eyes behold the inhabited world; *
his piercing eye weighs our worth.
6 The Lord weighs the righteous
as well as the wicked, *
but those who delight in violence he abhors.
7 Upon the wicked he shall rain coals of fire
and burning sulphur; *
a scorching wind shall be their lot.
8 For the Lord is righteous;
he delights in righteous deeds; *
and the just shall see his face.

Psalm 12 *Salvum me fac*

1 Help me, Lord, for there is no godly one left; *
the faithful have vanished from among us.
2 Everyone speaks falsely with their neighbour; *
with a smooth tongue
they speak from a double heart.
3 O that the Lord would cut off
all smooth tongues, *
and close the lips that utter proud boasts!
4 Those who say, "With our tongue will we prevail; *
our lips are our own; who is lord over us?"
5 "Because the needy are oppressed,
and the poor cry out in misery, *
I will rise up," says the Lord,
"and give them the help they long for."
6 The words of the Lord are pure words, *
like silver refined from ore
and purified seven times in the fire.
7 O Lord, watch over us *
and save us from this generation for ever.
8 The wicked prowl on every side, *
and that which is worthless
is highly prized by everyone.

A Song of Hope

1 God works for good in everything
with those who love him *
who are called according to his purpose.

2 For those whom he foreknew *
he also predestined to be conformed
to the image of his Son.

3 And those whom he predestined he also called *
and those whom he called he also justified.

4 And to those whom he justified *
he has also given his splendour.

5 If God is on our side *
who can ever be against us?

6 He who did not spare his own Son
but gave him up for us all *
will he not also with him freely give us all things?

7 It is God who justifies *
who then can ever condemn us?

8 For it is Christ Jesus who died
and was raised from the dead *
who is at God's right hand to plead our cause.

9 What can separate us from the love of Christ *
can persecution or hunger, can peril or the sword?

10 No, in all these things
we are more than conquerors *
through him who loved us,
even Jesus Christ our Lord.

Romans 8.28-35,37

Luke 23.33–43

And when they came to the place which is called The Skull, there they crucified him, and the criminals, one on the right and one on the left. And Jesus said, "Father, forgive them; for they know not what they do." And they cast lots to divide his garments. And the people stood by, watching; but the rulers scoffed at him, saying, "He saved others; let him save himself, if he is the Christ of God, his Chosen One!" The soldiers also mocked him, coming up and offering him vinegar, and saying, "If you are the King of the Jews, save yourself!" There was also an inscription over him, "This is the King of the Jews." One of the criminals who were hanged railed at him, saying, "Are you not the Christ? Save yourself and us!" But the other rebuked him, saying, "Do you not fear God, since you are under the same sentence of condemnation? And we indeed justly; for we are receiving the due reward of our deeds; but this man has done nothing wrong." And he said, "Jesus, remember me when you come into your kingdom." And he said to him, "Truly, I say to you, today you will be with me in Paradise."

John 19.23–30

When the soldiers had crucified Jesus they took his garments and made four parts, one for each soldier; also his tunic. But the tunic was without seam, woven from top to bottom; so they said to one another, "Let us not tear it, but cast lots for it to see whose it shall be." This was to fulfil the scripture, "They parted my garments among them, and for my clothing they cast lots." So the soldiers did this. But standing by the cross of Jesus were his mother, and his mother's sister, Mary the wife of Clopas, and Mary Magdalene. When Jesus saw his mother, and the disciple whom he loved standing near, he said to his mother, "Woman, behold, your son!" Then he said to the disciple, "Behold, your mother!" And from that hour the disciple took her to his own home. After this Jesus, knowing that all was now finished, said (to fulfil the scripture), "I thirst." A bowl full of vinegar stood there; so they put a sponge full of the vinegar on hyssop and held it to his mouth. When Jesus had received the vinegar, he said, "It is finished"; and he bowed his head and gave up his spirit.

Lord Jesus Christ, Son of the living God,
who at this evening hour lay in the tomb
and so hallowed the grave
to be a bed of hope
for all who put their trust in you:
give us such sorrow for our sins,
which were the cause of your passion,
that, when our bodies lie in the dust
our souls may live with you;
for you live and reign with the Father
and the Holy Spirit,
one God, now and ever. Amen.

Our Father…

To the only God, immortal, invisible,
be glory in the Church and in Christ Jesus,
for ever and ever. Amen.

Saturday Morning

O Lord open our lips.
  And our mouth shall proclaim your praise.

Hymn *Immortal, invisible*

Immortal, invisible, God only wise,
In light inaccessible hid from our eyes,
Most blessèd, most glorious,
    the Ancient of Days,
Almighty, victorious, thy great name we praise.

Unresting, unhasting, and silent as light,
Nor wanting, nor wasting, thou rulest in might;
Thy justice, like mountains, high soaring above
Thy clouds which are fountains
    of goodness and love.

Great Father of glory, pure Father of light,
Thine angels adore thee, all veiling their sight;
All laud we would render; O help us to see
'Tis only the splendour of light hideth thee.

Psalm 84 *Quam dilecta!*

1 How dear to me is your dwelling,
O Lord of hosts! *
My soul has a desire and longing
for the courts of the Lord;
my heart and my flesh rejoice
in the living God.

2 The sparrow has found her a house
and the swallow a nest
where she may lay her young; *
by the side of your altars, O Lord of hosts,
my King and my God.

3 Happy are they who dwell in your house! *
they will always be praising you.

4 Happy are the people whose strength is in you! *
whose hearts are set on the pilgrims' way.

5 Those who go through the desolate valley
will find it a place of springs, *
for the early rains have covered it
with pools of water.

6 They will climb from height to height, *
and the God of gods will reveal himself in Zion.

7 Lord God of hosts, hear my prayer; *
hearken, O God of Jacob.

8 Behold our defender, O God; *
and look upon the face of your anointed.

9 For one day in your courts is better than
a thousand in my own room, ⋆
and to stand at the threshold of the house
of my God than to dwell in the tents
of the wicked.
10 For the Lord God is both sun and shield; ⋆
he will give grace and glory;
11 No good thing will the Lord withhold ⋆
from those who walk with integrity.
12 O Lord of hosts, ⋆
happy are they who put their trust in you!

A Song of Humility

1 Christ Jesus was in the form of God ⋆
but he did not cling to equality with God.
2 He emptied himself,
taking the form of a servant, ⋆
and was born in the likeness of men;
3 And being found in human form ⋆
he humbled himself:
4 And became obedient unto death ⋆
even death on a cross.
5 Therefore God has highly exalted him ⋆
and bestowed on him the Name
above every name.

6 That at the name of Jesus
    every knee should bow *
  in heaven and on earth and under the earth.

7 And every tongue confess
    that Jesus Christ is Lord *
  to the glory of God the Father.

Philippians 2.6–11

Mark 15.42–16.1

And when evening had come, since it was the day of Preparation, that is, the day before the sabbath, Joseph of Arimathea, a respected member of the council, who was also himself looking for the kingdom of God, took courage and went to Pilate, and asked for the body of Jesus. And Pilate wondered if he were already dead; and summoning the centurion, he asked him whether he was already dead. And when he learned from the centurion that he was dead, he granted the body to Joseph. And he bought a linen shroud, and taking him down, wrapped him in the linen shroud, and laid him in a tomb which had been hewn out of the rock; and he rolled a stone against the door of the tomb. Mary Magdalene and Mary the mother of Joses saw where he was laid. And when the sabbath was past, Mary Magdalene, and Mary the mother of James, and Salome, bought spices, so that they might go and anoint him.

Revelation 12.7–12

Now war arose in heaven, Michael and his angels fighting against the dragon; and the dragon and his angels fought, but they were defeated and there was no longer any place for them in heaven. And the great dragon was thrown down, that ancient serpent, who is called the Devil and Satan, the deceiver of the whole world—he was thrown down to the earth, and his angels were thrown down with him. And I heard a loud voice in heaven, saying, "Now the salvation and the power and the kingdom of our God and the authority of his Christ have come, for the accuser of our brethren has been thrown down, who accuses them day and night before our God. And they have conquered him by the blood of the Lamb and by the word of their testimony, for they loved not their lives even unto death. Rejoice then, O heaven and you that dwell therein! But woe to you, O earth and sea, for the devil has come down to you in great wrath, because he knows that his time is short!"

Almighty God, Father of all mercies,
we your unworthy servants
give you most humble and hearty thanks
for all your goodness and loving-kindness
to us and to all people.
We bless you for our creation, preservation,
and all the blessings of this life;
but above all for your immeasurable love
in the redemption of the world
by our Lord Jesus Christ, for the means of grace
and for the hope of glory.
And give us, we pray, such a sense
of all your mercies, that our hearts
may be unfeignedly thankful,
and that we show forth your praise
not only with our lips but in our lives,
by giving ourselves to your service,
and by walking before you in holiness
and righteousness all our days;
through Jesus Christ our Lord, to whom,
with you and the Holy Spirit, be all honour
and glory, for ever and ever. Amen.

Our Father...

The grace of our Lord Jesus Christ
and the love of God
and the fellowship of the Holy Spirit
be with us all, evermore. Amen.

Saturday Evening

O God make speed to save us.
 O Lord make haste to help us.

Hymn *The day thou gavest*

The day thou gavest, Lord, is ended,
The darkness falls at thy behest;
To thee our morning hymns ascended,
Thy praise shall sanctify our rest.

We thank thee that thy Church unsleeping,
While earth rolls onward into light,
Through all the world her watch is keeping,
And rests not now by day or night.

The sun that bids us rest is waking
Our brethren 'neath the western sky,
And hour by hour fresh lips are making
Thy wondrous doings heard on high.

So be it, Lord; thy throne shall never,
Like earth's proud empires, pass away;
Thy kingdom stands, and grows for ever,
Till all thy creatures own thy sway.

Psalm 118 *Confitemini Domino*

1 Give thanks to the Lord, for he is good; *
his mercy endures for ever.

2 Let Israel now proclaim, *
"His mercy endures for ever."

3 Let the house of Aaron now proclaim, *
"His mercy endures for ever."

4 Let those who fear the Lord now proclaim, *
"His mercy endures for ever."

5 I called to the Lord in my distress; *
the Lord answered by setting me free.

6 The Lord is at my side, therefore I will not fear; *
what can anyone do to me?

7 The Lord is at my side to help me; *
I will triumph over those who hate me.

8 It is better to rely on the Lord *
than to put any trust in flesh.

9 It is better to rely on the Lord *
than to put any trust in rulers.

10 All the ungodly encompass me; *
in the name of the Lord I will repel them.

11 They hem me in, they hem me in on every side; *
in the name of the Lord I will repel them.

12 They swarm about me like bees;
they blaze like a fire of thorns; *
in the name of the Lord I will repel them.

13 I was pressed so hard that I almost fell, *
but the Lord came to my help.
14 The Lord is my strength and my song, *
and he has become my salvation.
15 There is a sound of exultation and victory *
in the tents of the righteous:
16 "The right hand of the Lord has triumphed!
the right hand of the Lord is exalted! *
the right hand of the Lord has triumphed!"

The Song of Moses

1 I will sing to the Lord for his glorious triumph; *
the horse and the rider
he has hurled into the sea.
2 The Lord has become my strength and refuge; *
the Lord himself has become my saviour.
3 He is my God and I will praise him; *
my father's God and I will exalt him.
4 The Lord himself is a mighty warrior; *
the Lord, the Lord is his name.
5 Your right hand, O Lord, is majestic in power; *
your right hand, O Lord, shatters the enemy.
6 Who is like you, O Lord, among the gods, *
holy, awesome, worker of wonders?

7 In steadfast love you led your people, *
you guided your redeemed
with your great strength.

8 You brought them safely to your holy place, *
and planted them firm
on your own mountain.

9 You brought them into your own house. *
The Lord shall reign for ever and ever.

Exodus 15.1–3,6,11,17–18

John 4.7–15

There came a woman of Samaria to draw water. Jesus said to her, "Give me a drink." For his disciples had gone away into the city to buy food. The Samaritan woman said to him, "How is it that you, a Jew, ask a drink of me, a woman of Samaria?" For Jews have no dealings with Samaritans. Jesus answered her, "If you knew the gift of God, and who it is that is saying to you, 'Give me a drink,' you would have asked him, and he would have given you living water." The woman said to him, "Sir, you have nothing to draw with, and the well is deep; where do you get that living water? Are you greater than our father Jacob, who gave us the well, and drank from it himself, and his sons, and his cattle?" Jesus said to her, "Every one who drinks of this water will thirst again, but whoever drinks of the water that I shall give him will never thirst; the water that I shall give him will become in him a spring of water welling up to eternal life." The woman said to him, "Sir, give me this water, that I may not thirst, nor come here to draw."

John 11.28–44

When she had said this, she went and called her sister Mary, saying quietly, "The Teacher is here and is calling for you." And when she heard it, she rose quickly and went to him. Now Jesus had not yet come to the village, but was still in the place where Martha had met him. When the Jews who were with her in the house, consoling her, saw Mary rise quickly and go out, they followed her, supposing that she was going to the tomb to weep there. Then Mary, when she came where Jesus was and saw him, fell at his feet, saying to him, "Lord, if you had been here, my brother would not have died." When Jesus saw her weeping, and the Jews who came with her also weeping, he was deeply moved in spirit and troubled; and he said, "Where have you laid him?" They said to him, "Lord, come and see." Jesus wept. So the Jews said, "See how he loved him!" But some of them said, "Could not he who opened the eyes of the blind man have kept this man from dying?" Then Jesus, deeply moved again, came to the tomb; it was a cave, and a stone lay upon it. Jesus said, "Take away the stone." Martha, the sister of the dead man, said to him, "Lord, by this time there will be an odour, for he has been dead four days." Jesus said to her, "Did I not tell you that if you would believe you would see the glory of God?" So they took away the stone. And Jesus lifted up his eyes and said, "Father, I thank thee that thou hast heard me. I knew that thou hearest me always, but I have said this on account of the people standing by, that they may believe that thou didst send me." When he had said this, he cried with a loud voice, "Lazarus, come out." The dead man came out, his hands and feet bound with bandages, and his face wrapped with a cloth. Jesus said to them, "Unbind him, and let him go."

Come to visit us, O God, this night,
so that by your strength
we may rise with the new day
to rejoice in the resurrection of your Son,
Jesus Christ our Lord;
who lives and reigns with you
and the Holy Spirit, one God,
now and for ever. Amen.

Our Father…

To the only God, immortal, invisible,
be glory in the Church and in Christ Jesus,
for ever and ever. Amen.

Plainsong Hymns

Sunday Morning *VI*

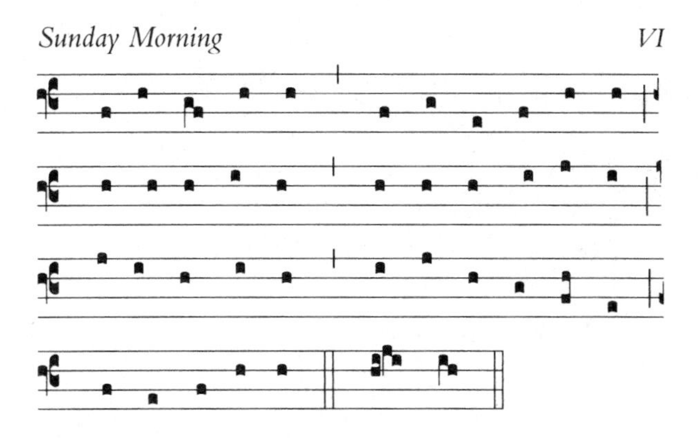

Father, we praise you, now the night is over,
Active and watchful, stand we all before you;
Singing, we offer prayer and adoration:
Thus we adore you.

Monarch of all things, fit us for your kingdom;
Banish our weakness,
health and wholeness sending;
Bring us to heaven, where your saints united
Joy without ending.

All-holy Father, Son and equal Spirit,
Trinity blessed, send us your salvation;
Yours is the glory, filling all creation,
Ever resounding.

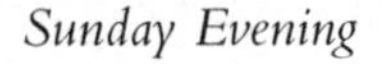

O Christ, the Church's glorious Head,
We praise you, first-born from the dead,
The image of our God brought low
That we divinity might know.

Through you and for you, at God's word,
The formless depths to life were stirred;
All things in heaven and on earth,
All sovereignties have come to birth.

In you God's fullness came to dwell,
That love might Satan's hold repel,
And by your death upon the tree
You loosed us from captivity.

To God the Father, God the Son.
And God the Spirit, Three in One,
To you, O blessed Trinity,
Be praise in all eternity.

CSMV Wantage, alt.

Monday Morning *I*

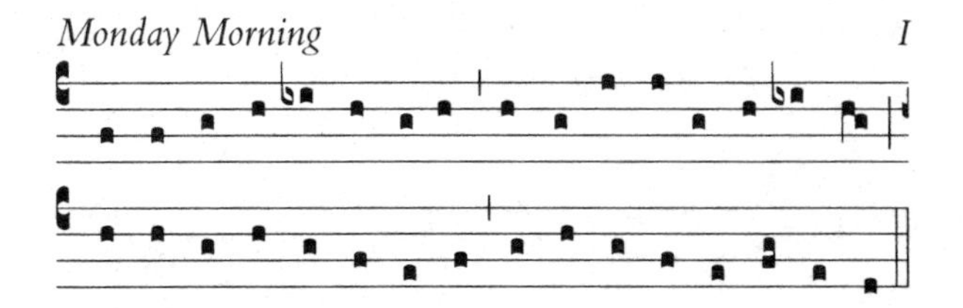

O God of light, the dawning day
Gives us new promise of your love.
Each fresh beginning is your gift,
Like gentle dew from heaven above.

Your blessings, Father, never fail:
Your Son, who is our daily bread,
The Holy Spirit of your love,
By whom each day your Church is led.

Make us the servants of your peace,
Renew our strength, remove all fear;
Be with us, Lord, throughout this day,
For all is joy if you are near.

To Father, Son and Spirit blest,
One only God, we humbly pray;
Show us the splendour of your light
In death, the dawn of perfect day.

James Quinn SJ

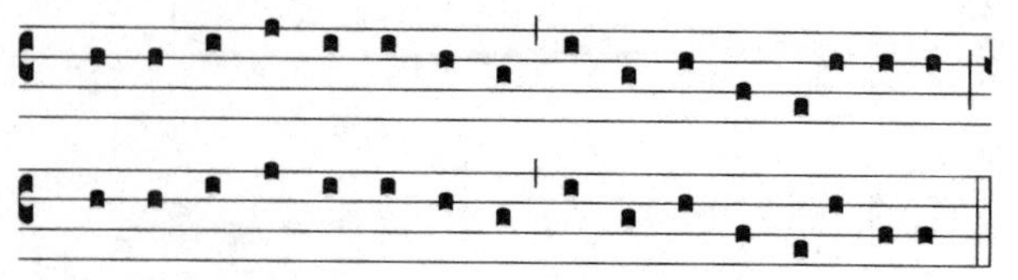

O boundless wisdom, God most high,
Creator of the earth and sky,
With rushing streams and glistening rain
All living creatures you sustain.

The clouds above the earth you raised
Lest sun's fierce heat should scorch and waste.
The floods you hold restrained below
Lest raging chaos overflow.

So pour on us who seek your face,
The waters of your quickening grace;
Renew the source of life within,
Wash from our souls the stain of sin.

Let faith discern th' eternal light
Beyond the darkness of the night,
That through the glass we darkly see
The way of truth which sets us free.

To God the Father, God the Son,
And God the Spirit, ever One,
All honour, praise and glory be
From age to age eternally.

Tuesday Morning *IV*

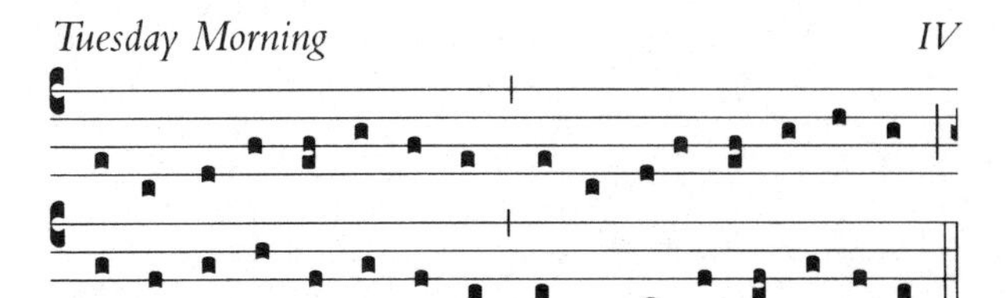

Light of our darkness, Word of God,
Sent to illumine earthly night,
You we salute with singing hearts,
Bathed in the splendour of your light.

Sword that can pierce the inmost soul,
Stripping whatever thoughts are there,
Cut to the marrow of our minds;
Enter our hearts and lay them bare.

Vessel of God's abundant life,
Bearer of truth that sets us free,
Breaking the deadly grasp of sin,
Work in our hearts your mystery.

Word that has overcome the world,
Seed of immortal destiny,
Grow in our hearts, that we may live
Sharing your deathless victory.

Creator of the sea and land,
Almighty Lord, at your command,
The stormy deeps give way to earth,
A sign of coming life and birth.

Each living branch, each fruit and seed
Tells in itself a godly deed:
The green trees blossom and fulfil,
In bearing fruit, your perfect will.

Lord, heal the wounds through sin sustained,
That we in faith and hope regained,
May find for penance true a place
And know the strength and life of grace.

May every soul your law obey
And keep from every evil way;
Rejoice each promised good to win
And flee from every mortal sin.

To God the Father, God the Son,
And God the Spirit, ever One,
All honour, praise and glory be
From age to age eternally.

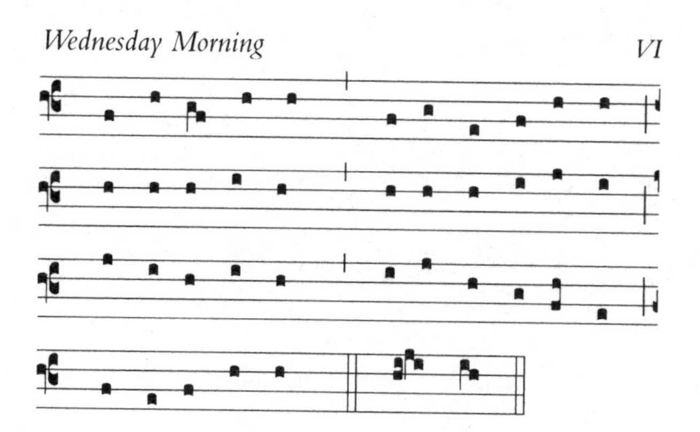

See, now the shadows of the night are fading,
Sunlight arising, dawn of day in splendour;
Spirit enlightened, to the mighty Father,
Pray we devoutly.

That in his mercy he may always keep us,
Eager and ready for his holy service;
Then may he give us, of a father's goodness,
Joy in his kingdom.

This may he grant us, God for ever blessed,
Father eternal, Son and Holy Spirit:
His is the glory, filling all creation,
Ever resounding.

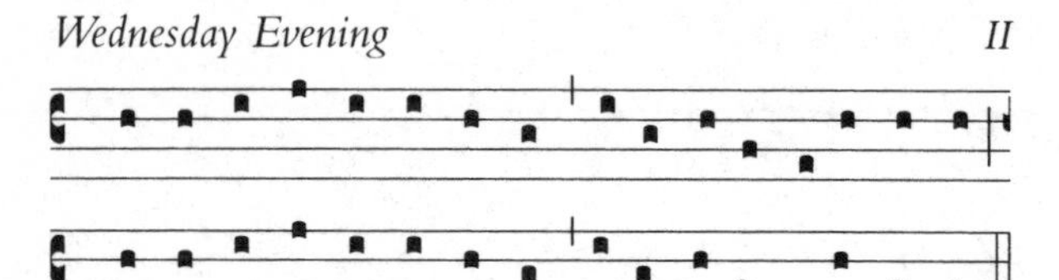

O God, whose hand has spread the sky
With all its shining hosts on high,
And, when the fourth day was begun,
Did frame the circle of the sun.

Endowing it with fiery light,
You crowned the sun with royal might,
And set the moon her ordered ways
To mark and govern months and days.

Shed forth your truth, O Fount of light,
In Christ the Way lead us aright;
As children bright with your new fire,
Come, Lord, fulfil our heart's desire.

To God the Father, God the Son,
And God the Spirit, ever One,
All honour, praise and glory be
From age to age eternally.

Thursday Morning *I*

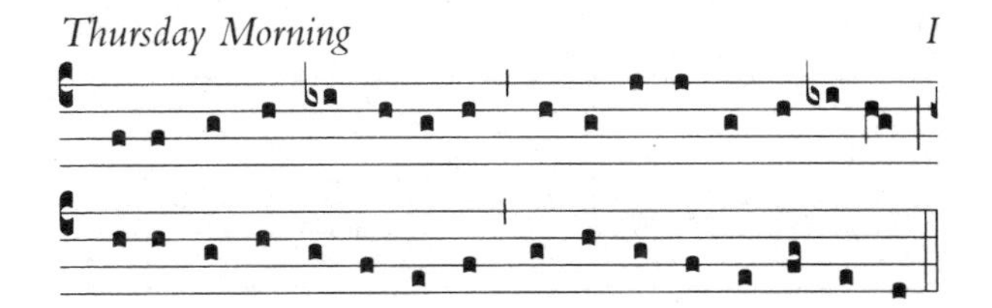

The beauty of the rising sun,
Begins to flood the world with light;
Awakened, nature glows with life
In form and colour true and bright.

Lord Jesus Christ, since time began
The morning sun you far outshone;
We turn to you with joyous praise
And ask the blessings you have won.

You are God's knowledge infinite,
His Word that brought all things to be:
Answer our prayer that we may love
And come to see your mystery

Give us your light, that we may learn
To walk the path of life with care;
May all our ways and actions show
The gifts the Father longs to share.

Most loving Father, hear our prayer
Through Jesus Christ, your only Son;
Who with the Holy Spirit reign
For ever Three and ever One.

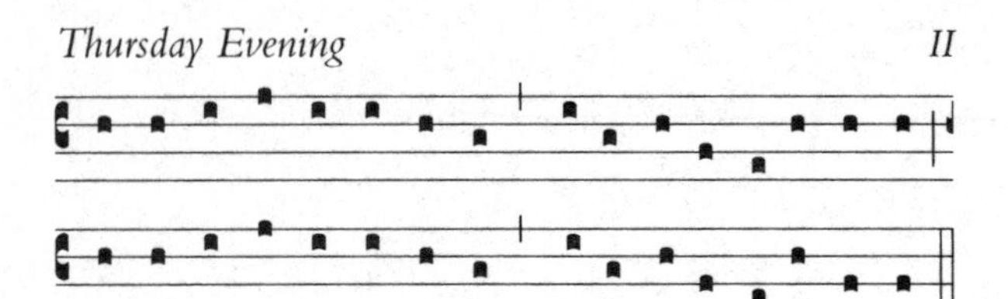

Creator of life's mystery,
From nothing bringing all to be;
The skies, the sea, and earth below,
Now filled with life, your glory show.

You set the fish to swim the sea,
And birds in open air to be,
That each by origin the same,
Its separate dwelling place might claim.

Grant that your people, by the tide
Of blood and water purified,
No guilty fall from you may know,
Nor death eternal undergo.

But in that water here reborn,
May we in hope await the morn—
When, by your grace our service done,
We rise triumphant in the Son.

Almighty Father, hear our cry
Through Jesus Christ our Lord most high,
Whom in the Spirit we adore,
Who reigns with you for evermore.

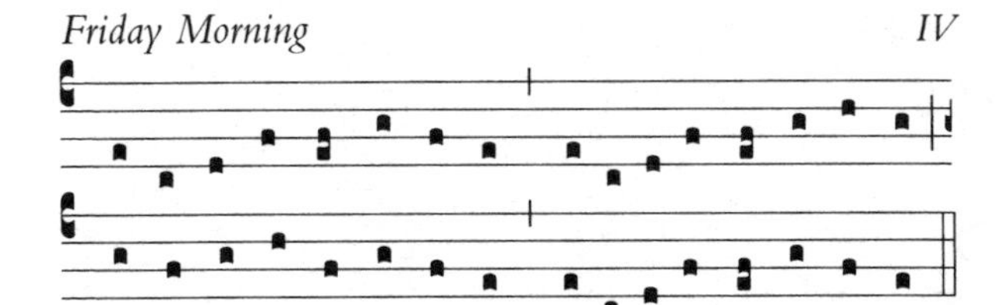

Eternal glory fills the heaven,
Our only hope, in mercy given:
Christ Jesus, whom a virgin bore,
Son of the Father evermore.

The morning star shines bright and clear
Announcing that the day is near.
Lord, grant us strength our hearts to raise,
That we this day may sing your praise.

Night's shadows flee: Lord, on us shine;
Our darkness turn to light divine;
Then in that light our life may rest,
Renewed by grace, and by you blest.

Let faith assume the foremost part,
Be firmly rooted in the heart;
And joyous hope in second place,
Then love may reign, your greatest grace.

All glory to the Father be,
And to the Son, eternally;
And to the Spirit, equal praise
From joyful hearts we ever raise.

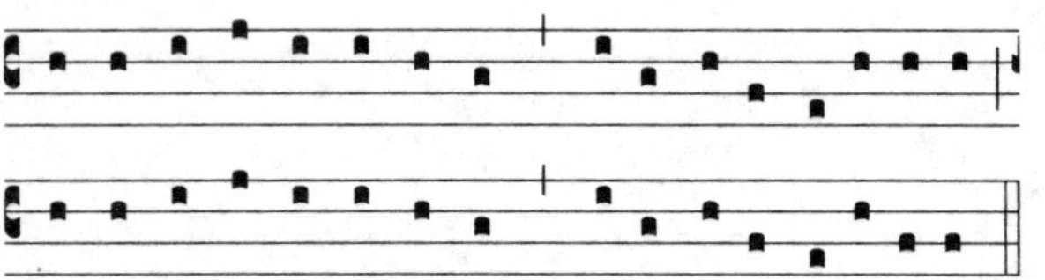

Our Lord and Maker, from your throne,
You fashion all things, God alone;
At your decree the living earth
To creatures great and small gave birth.

From all your servants drive away
Whatever sinful thoughts today
Disturbed th' intentions of the heart
Or in our actions claimed their part.

In heaven your endless joys bestow,
And grant your gifts of grace below;
From chains of strife our souls release,
Bind fast the gentle bands of peace.

To God the Father, God the Son,
And God the Spirit, ever One,
All honour, praise and glory be
From age to age eternally.

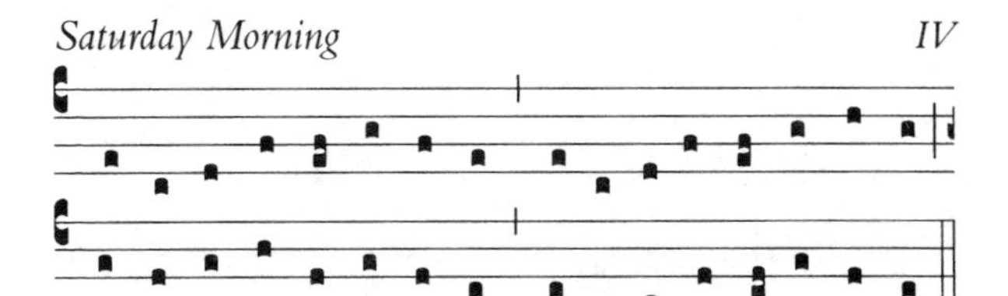

The light of morning fills the sky,
In golden dawn day lays its claim:
Swift climbing, searching shafts of light,
Dispelling darkness, sin and shame.

Away, all unreality,
Away, despair born of the night!
The fear and guilt that dark creates
The light has banished from our sight.

So, Lord, when that last morning breaks
For which, while here, we long and pray;
Then may it to your people prove
The dawning of your glorious day.

To God the Father, glory be,
And to his well-beloved Son,
Who with the Spirit dwell in us:
Immortal Trinity in One.

O Trinity of blessed light,
O Unity of primal might,
Th' untiring sun now goes its way;
Shed now within our hearts your ray.

To you our morning song of praise,
To you our evening prayer we raise;
Your glory suppliant we adore
For ever and for evermore.

To God the Father, God the Son
And God the Spirit, praise be done;
To you most holy Trinity
Praise now and for eternity.

Loving Creator turn and hear
The cries and prayers, with many a tear
Poured forth by all the penitent
Who keep this holy fast of Lent.

Our hearts to you are open, Lord,
And all our weakness you record;
Pour out on all who seek your face
Abundance of your pardoning grace.

Spare us, good Lord, who now confess
Our sinful ways and wickedness,
And for the glory of your name,
Our fainting souls to life reclaim.

Give us the discipline that springs
From abstinence in outward things;
That we, while fasting inwardly,
In heart and soul with you may be.

Grant us, O blessed Trinity,
One God, unchanging Unity,
That this our fast of forty days
Bear fruit in penitence and praise.

From east to west, from shore to shore,
Let every heart awake and sing
The holy child whom Mary bore,
The Christ, the everlasting King.

Behold, the world's creator wears
The form and fashion of a slave;
Our very flesh our maker shares,
His fallen creature, man, to save.

From heav'n a mighty gift of grace
Within the Virgin Mother flows;
Her womb becomes the secret place
That bears the Lord who all things knows.

She bowed her to the angel's word,
Declaring what the Father willed;
And suddenly the promised Lord
That pure and hallowed temple filled.

And while the angels in the sky
Sang praise above the silent field,
To shepherds poor the Lord most high,
The one great Shepherd, was revealed.

All praise to you, Incarnate Son,
And endless glory ever be!
With Father and with Spirit one,
Be praise through all eternity. Amen.

Christmas *I*

O Christ, Redeemer of us all,
Before the earliest dawn of light
From everlasting ages born,
Immense in glory and in might.

Immortal hope of all mankind,
In whom the Father's face we see;
Lord, hear your people's prayers today,
Receive from all the world our plea.

Remember, O our saving Lord,
How in the virgin undefiled,
You took the form of humankind
And in our flesh became a child.

This ever-blest recurring day
Its witness bears that you, alone
Salvation's source, yourself leapt down
From God the Father's heavenly throne.

O day, to which the seas and sky
And earth and stars glad welcome sing;
O day which healed our misery
And brought to earth salvation's King.

From sin made clean and marked for God,
On this the day that saw your birth,
This people bought by your dear blood,
Sing high the song of ransomed earth.

To you, Lord Jesus, virgin-born,
Immortal glory ever be!
With Father and with Spirit blest,
All holy, glorious Trinity.

Star of sea and ocean,
Gateway to man's heaven,
Mother of our maker,
Hear our prayer, O Maiden.

Welcoming the Ave
Of God's simple greeting
You have borne a Saviour
Far beyond all dreaming.

Loose the bonds that hold us
Bound in sin's own blindness
That with eyes now opened
God's own light may guide us.

Show yourself our mother
He will hear your pleading
Whom your womb has sheltered
And whose hand brings healing.

Gentlest of all virgins,
That our love be faithful
Keep us from all evil
Gentle, strong and grateful.

Guard us through life's dangers
Never turn and leave us,
May our hope find harbour
In the calm of Jesus.

Sing to God our Father
Through the Son who saves us
Joyful in the Spirit
Everlasting praises. Amen.

Ralph Wright OSB

Sing high the song of Life and Love
Throughout a world that sin had won;
Redemption is the Father's gift
Bestowed on us by Mary's Son.

That which Isaiah prophesied
The faithful Virgin has fulfilled;
And what the angel's word began
The Holy Spirit's love has sealed.

Believing in th' angelic word
A mother's joy did Mary gain;
Her virgin-womb became the shrine
Of him whom earth could not contain.

The guilt so long by Adam borne
The Second Adam washed away;
What Adam's pride had cast aside
The humble Lord restores today.

All glory be to Christ the Lord
In whom we see the Father's face;
Whom blessed Mary gently bore,
A mother by the Spirit's grace.

O holy Mary, brighter far
Than any burning, shining star:
From your Creator you were given
The grace to bear the King of heaven.

As second Eve, you brought to birth
The second Adam for this earth;
All evil powers he overthrew,
In him we all are born anew.

You were the gate of heaven's high Lord,
The door through which the Light has poured:
Christians, rejoice that Mary's word
Brought life and grace in Christ our Lord.

O Jesus, Virgin-born, we raise
To you our hymn of grateful praise;
And to the Father tribute bring,
As by the Spirit here we sing. Amen.

Additional Prayers

For the Fraternity

Almighty God,
who through your only-begotten Son
Jesus Christ overcame death and opened to us
the gate of everlasting life: we humbly beseech
you that, as by your special grace
going before us you put into our minds
good desires, so by your continued help
we may bring them to good effect;
through Jesus Christ our Lord, who lives
and reigns with you and the Holy Spirit,
one God, now and for ever. Amen.

For the College

O God and Father of us all,
you send labourers into your vineyard:
set on fire many hearts with a sense
of their vocation and with an eager response
to your call, and to those whom you have
gathered at the College of the Resurrection
give grace to prepare in all earnestness and zeal,
that with entire consecration of heart and life
they may labour hereafter in your holy Church;
through Jesus Christ our Lord, who lives
and reigns with you and the Holy Spirit,
one God, now and for ever. Amen.

For the Community

Almighty and everlasting God,
who formed your Church to be of one heart
and one soul in the power of the Resurrection
and the fellowship of the Holy Spirit:
renew her evermore in her first love;
and grant such a measure thereof
to the brethren of the Resurrection,
that their life may be hallowed,
their way directed, and their work
made fruitful, to the good of your Church
and the glory of your holy name;
through Jesus Christ our Lord. Amen.

For the Church

Most gracious Father, we humbly pray
for the holy Catholic Church.
Fill it with all truth, in all truth with all peace.
Where it is corrupt, purge it;
where it is in error, direct it;
where anything is amiss, reform it;
where it is right, strengthen and confirm it;
where it is in want, furnish it;
where it is divided and rent asunder,
make up the breaches of it,
O Holy One of Israel. Amen.

For all Christian people

Almighty and everlasting God,
by whose Spirit the whole body of the Church
is governed and sanctified: hear our prayer
which we offer for all your faithful people;
that each in their vocation and ministry
may serve you in holiness and truth
to the glory of your name;
through our Lord and Saviour Jesus Christ. Amen.

For vocations

Almighty God,
you have entrusted to your Church
a share in the ministry of your Son,
our great High Priest.
Inspire by your Holy Spirit
the hearts and minds of many
to offer themselves for the sacred ministry,
that as deacons and priests
they may draw all people to your kingdom;
through Jesus Christ our Lord. Amen.

For religious communities

Almighty God, as you have led men
and women in this and every age to bind
themselves in religious communities
for your single service: accept their oblation
and hallow their common life,
that with your whole Church
they may press forward to the more perfect
obedience of your Son,
Jesus Christ our Lord. Amen.

For religious communities

O Lord, who called Peter, James and John
to be with you in your agony
in Gethsemane, call many now,
both men and women
to share the like privilege of the Religious Life;
that through watching and prayer
they may come to see the vision of your glory
and so proclaim your praise and honour
in a world made new in your risen life;
for with the Father and the Holy Spirit
you alone are our God,
now and for ever. Amen.

Finding God in all things

EACH DAY, perhaps at midday or in the evening, it is a good thing to reflect over the day and see how we have answered the call of God to love him and serve him in every part of our lives. This helps us to see more clearly where God is usually to be found and gives us confidence that he is with us wherever we are. This exercise can be done anywhere and only takes a few minutes. It consists of five steps:

God gives me life

Everything I have comes from God. Without him I have nothing, am nothing. Everything I see, the beauty, the friends and the life within me comes as a gift from God. I am utterly poor but God makes me rich. So I let thankfulness for God's goodness rise up within me.

God, send me your Spirit

As I look over the day I need the Holy Spirit to show me where God has been. In a few words I ask for that grace.

God in all things

I let my mind wander over the day, recalling things I have seen, people I have spoken with, feelings that have come to me. Have I seen God in each of these? Have I responded generously or have I turned away from him? I remember and experience again the feelings I have had—joy and sorrow, delight and boredom, fear and confidence, excitement and anger, irritation and affirmation. Do these tell me how I was answering the call of God in the people and the world around me? It is good to remember the moments of grace, the happiness or even the sadness when God was in it. The world comes alive and people are seen as children of God bringing him to us.

God, I am sorry

I may remember silly things I have said, hurt I have given, and a failure to see God around me. I am sorry for that. Yet I give thanks too because God has been with me and I have often heard him and felt him and seen him in others. I pray for a deeper contrition and a greater thankfulness.

What next, God?

I look briefly at the rest of the day and tomorrow. Where may I expect to see God? I go out into my day in confidence that God will be with me. How can I serve him and show him my love?

Compline

The Lord Almighty grant us a quiet night
and a perfect end.
Amen.

A period of silence follows for reflection on the past day.

We confess * to almighty God,
before the whole company of heaven
and one another, that we have sinned
through our own fault, in thought and word
and deed, and in what we have failed to do.
Wherefore, we pray almighty God
to forgive us our sins and to keep us
in eternal life. Amen.

Our help is in the name of the Lord.
Who has made heaven and earth.

Glory to the Father, and to the Son,
and to the Holy Spirit:
as it was in the beginning, is now,
and shall be for ever. Amen.

Alleluia. *(not in Lent)*

Psalm 4 *Cum invocarem*

1 Answer me when I call, O God,
defender of my cause; *
you set me free when I am hard-pressed;
have mercy on me and hear my prayer.

2 "You mortals,
how long will you dishonour my glory; *
how long will you worship dumb idols
and run after false gods?"

3 Know that the Lord does wonders
for the faithful; *
when I call upon the Lord, he will hear me.

4 Tremble, then, and do not sin; *
speak to your heart in silence upon your bed.

5 Offer the appointed sacrifices *
and put your trust in the Lord.

6 Many are saying, "Oh, that we might see
better times!" *
Lift up the light of your countenance
upon us, O Lord.

7 You have put gladness in my heart, *
more than when grain and wine and oil increase.

8 I lie down in peace; at once I fall asleep; *
for only you, Lord, make me dwell in safety.

Psalm 91 *Qui habitat*

1 He who dwells in the shelter of the Most High, *
abides under the shadow of the Almighty.

2 He shall say to the Lord,
"You are my refuge and my stronghold, *
my God in whom I put my trust."

3 He shall deliver you from the snare of the hunter *
and from the deadly pestilence.

4 He shall cover you with his pinions,
and you shall find refuge under his wings; *
his faithfulness shall be a shield and buckler.

5 You shall not be afraid of any terror by night, *
nor of the arrow that flies by day.

6 Of the plague that stalks in the darkness, *
nor of the sickness that lays waste at mid-day.

7 A thousand shall fall at your side
and ten thousand at your right hand, *
but it shall not come near you.

8 Your eyes have only to behold *
to see the reward of the wicked.

9 Because you have made the Lord your refuge, *
and the Most High your habitation.

10 There shall no evil happen to you, *
neither shall any plague
come near your dwelling.

11 For he shall give his angels charge over you, *
to keep you in all your ways.

12 They shall bear you in their hands, *
lest you dash your foot against a stone.
13 You shall tread upon the lion and adder; *
you shall trample the young lion
and the serpent under your feet.
14 Because he is bound to me in love,
therefore will I deliver him; *
I will protect him, because he knows my name.
15 He shall call upon me, and I will answer him; *
I am with him in trouble; I will rescue him
and bring him to honour.
16 With long life will I satisfy him, *
and show him my salvation.

Psalm 134 *Ecce nunc*

1 Behold now, bless the Lord,
all you servants of the Lord, *
you that stand by night
in the house of the Lord.
2 Lift up your hands in the holy place
and bless the Lord; *
the Lord who made heaven and earth
bless you out of Zion.

Sunday
The servants of the Lamb shall see the face of their God, whose name will be on their foreheads. There will be no more night: they will not need the light of a lamp or the light of the sun, for God will give them light; and they will reign for ever and ever.

Revelation 22.4,5

or

There remains a sabbath rest for the people of God; for those who enter his rest also cease from their labours, as he did. Let us, therefore, strive to enter that rest.

Hebrews 4.9–11

Monday
In returning and rest you shall be saved; in quietness and trust shall be your strength.

Isaiah 30.15

Tuesday
Come to me, all who labour and are heavy laden, and I will give you rest. Take my yoke upon you and learn from me; for I am gentle and lowly in heart, and you will find rest for your souls. For my yoke is easy, and my burden is light.

Matthew 11.28–30

Wednesday

Humble yourselves under the mighty hand of God, that in due time he may exalt you. Cast all your anxieties on him, for he cares about you.

1 Peter 5.6,7

Thursday

The Word was the source of life, and brought life to all. The light shines in the darkness, and the darkness has not overcome it.

John 1.4,5

Friday

Lord, you are in the midst of us, and we are called by your name. Leave us not, O Lord our God.

Jeremiah 14.9

Saturday

There remains a sabbath rest for the people of God; for those who enter his rest also cease from their labours, as he did. Let us, therefore, strive to enter that rest.

Hebrews 4.9–11

Response

VI

and to the Holy Spirit.

Hymn

VIII

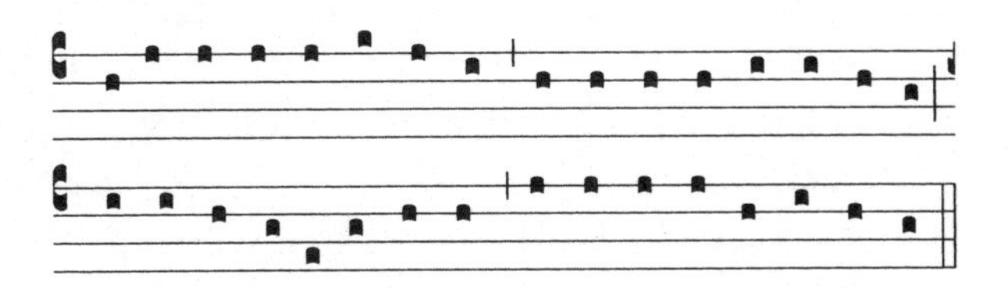

To you, before the end of day,
Creator of the world, we pray:
In love unfailing hear our prayer,
Enfold us in your watchful care.

Keep all disturbing dreams away,
And hold the evil foe at bay,
Repose untroubled let us find
For soul and body, heart and mind.

Almighty Father, hear our cry
Through Jesus Christ our Lord most high;
Who reigns with you eternally
In your blest Spirit's unity. Amen.

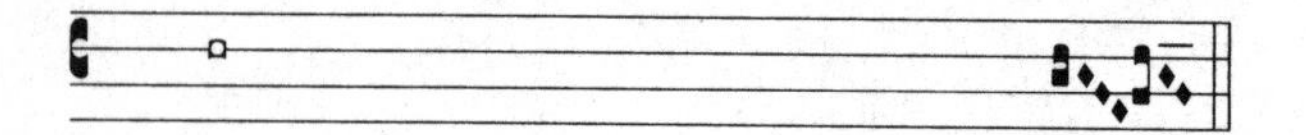

℣. Keep me, O Lord, as the apple of your eye, (alleluia).
℟. Hide me under the shadow of your wings, (alleluia).

Nunc Dimittis *IIIa*

Lord, now you let your sérvant depárt in peace *
your wórd has béen fulfilled.
My own eyes have séen the salvátion *
which you have prepared in the sight
of évery péople.
A light to reveal you tó the nátions *
and the glory of your péople Ísrael.
Glory to the Father, and to the Son,
and to the Hóly Spírit; *
as it was in the beginning,
is now, and shall be for éver. Ámen.

(The Antiphon is repeated)

Lord, have mercy
Christ, have mercy
Lord, have mercy

God raised him up from the dead
and gave him glory;
That our faith and hope might be in God.

Almighty and everlasting God,
who formed your Church
to be of one heart and one soul
in the power of the Resurrection
and the fellowship of the Holy Spirit:
renew her evermore in her first love;
and grant such a measure thereof
to the brethren of the Resurrection,
that their life may be hallowed,
their way directed,
and their work made fruitful,
to the good of your Church
and the glory of your holy name;
through Jesus Christ our Lord. Amen.

Visit, O Lord, this dwelling,
and drive away all snares of the enemy;
may the angels preserve us in peace,
and your blessing be ever upon us;
through Jesus Christ our Lord. Amen.

In peace, we will lie down and sleep;
For you alone, Lord, make us dwell in safety.

The almighty and merciful God,
the Father, the Son, and the Holy Spirit,
bless and preserve us. Amen.

Acknowledgements

The editors and Mirfield Publications thank the owners or controllers of copyright for permission to use the copyright material listed below. Every effort has been made to trace copyright owners, and the editors apologise to any whose rights have inadvertently not been acknowledged.

The Psalms and other extracts from *Celebrating Common Prayer* (Mowbray, 1992) are copyright © The European Province of the Society of Saint Francis 1992 and are reproduced with permission. The Psalmody was adapted by the Society from that in the *Standard Book of Common Prayer* of the Episcopal Church in the USA, on which no copyright is claimed.

Some of the prayers reproduced from *Celebrating Common Prayer* are by and copyright © The Right Reverend David Silk, and are reproduced by permission.

The Post Communion Prayer for Easter Day from *The Christian Year: Collects and Post Communion Prayers for Sundays and Festivals* (Church House Publishing, 1997) is copyright © The Archbishops' Council and is reproduced by permission.

The Benedictus, Magnificat and Nunc Dimittis from *The Alternative Service Book, 1980*, are copyright © The International Consultation on English Texts (International Consultation on English Texts). The Lord's Prayer in its modern form is adapted from the International Consultation on English Texts version. Reproduced by permission of the publishers.

Other extracts from *The Alternative Service Book*, are copyright © The Archbishops' Council and are reproduced by permission.

The Collect for Good Friday, used here for Friday morning, is adapted from *The Book of Common Prayer*, the rights in which are vested in the Crown, and is reproduced by permission of the Crown's patentee, the Cambridge University Press.

Additional thanks are due to The Canterbury Press, Norwich, publishers of the *New English Hymnal*, from which the texts of the hymns contained within the offices have been taken.

Μεγαλύνει ἡ ψυχή μου τὸν κύριον Luke 1.46